Two Dachshunds at Troy

Jeremy Lousada

PNEUMA SPRINGS PUBLISHING UK

First Published in 2011 by:
Pneuma Springs Publishing

Two Dachshunds at Troy - A dog's tale
Copyright © 2011   Jeremy Lousada

Jeremy Lousada has asserted his/her right under the Copyright, Designs and Patents Act, 1988, to be identified as Author of this Work

Pneuma Springs

British Library Cataloguing in Publication Data

Lousada, Jeremy.
  Two dachshunds at Troy : a dog's tale.
  1. Lousada, Jeremy. 2. Lousada, Jeremy--Travel. 3. Dog owners--Great Britain--Biography. 4. Dachshunds--Biography. 5. Human-animal relationships--Anecdotes.
  I. Title
  636.7'538'0929-dc22

ISBN-13: 9781907728204

Pneuma Springs Publishing
A Subsidiary of Pneuma Springs Ltd.
7 Groveherst Road, Dartford Kent, DA1 5JD.
E: admin@pneumasprings.co.uk
W: www.pneumasprings.co.uk

Published in the United Kingdom. All rights reserved under International Copyright Law. Contents and/or cover may not be reproduced in whole or in part without the express written consent of the publisher.

For Debbie, Nathan & Charlotte

Two Dachshunds at Troy

A dog's tale

with best wishes

Jeremy

For Jean with love

Chapter One

> *"Master this is thy servant. He is rising eight weeks old,*
> *He is mainly Head and Tummy. His legs are uncontrolled.*
> *But thou has forgiven his ugliness, and settled him on Thy knee,*
> *Art thou content with thy servant? He is very comfy with thee."*
>
> R. Kipling

This is a dog's tale, or rather a tale of two dogs, small dogs. Those of you who keep and love pet giraffes, baby crocodiles and cats need read no further. Small dogs they may be, and perhaps like Pooh, of small brain, but few can have had such adventurous lives. They were almost certainly the first dogs ever to cross Europe by water from the North Sea to the Black Sea, they walked on the same stones the Turkish fleet was tied on before Lepanto, they chased baboons in Africa, hunted rabbits in the High Jura and lizards in the ruins of Troy. What they thought of it all we cannot be sure, communications were generally good but not perfect. In some cases, such as Rommel's perplexity with sea water, the thought processes were obvious, in others the nuances of thought were beyond our communication levels and I have had to use some poetic licence. But let me start at the beginning.

She was born on the 9th of December 1984 in Highlands, a suburb of Harare, Zimbabwe.

Her father was high born of impeccable lineage, numbering champions among his forebears, and he himself, having championship pretensions. Her mother was an orphan and nothing is known of her maternal relations.

Their owner was my dentist.

Regretfully none of her vital statistics were recorded at birth, but I imagine they ran to about two inches in length and a couple of ounces.

I didn't see her until nearly the end of January 1985. She was to be the first new puppy in our household for nearly twenty years.

The reason for this had nothing to do with a want of dogs in our household, in fact the opposite. Zimbabwe abounded in maltreated strays and mongrels of a parentage which would have baffled the best judges at Crufts.

My home at the time suffered from a surfeit of females, including my wife Jean and daughters Alex and Sarah. All were addicted to animals. We never had time to start with puppies. Abandoned strays and starved juveniles came to their attention with monotonous regularity. Others swamped by female households, will understand the pressures involved, but for those of you who have escaped the tyranny I will give an example.

Jean and our next door neighbour's wife were chatting by the gate when an African passed dragging a very small cross bred Maltese poodle along by a piece of string. It was filthy, covered in sores and suffering from malnutrition.

Without considering what they would do with it subsequently, they launched themselves into action. The dog was seized, the owner threatened with prosecution unless he handed it over then and there, and finally five shillings changed hands to the complete satisfaction of the previous owner.

Left triumphantly holding a string with six pounds of dirty, tick infested misery at one end, they looked at each other in consternation. Only then did their respective husband's strictures on the collection of further strays come to mind!

They made one of those unprincipled pacts so dear to female logic. Whoever's husband returned home last would be presented with the specimen.

My daughters returned from school – 'poor dear little dog'.

One would think that the God of our destinies would reward honesty and hard labour. Had I been out drowning my day's labours in a bar, I could have understood it, but as it happened I was working late.

My arrival home was greeted with hugs.

'Poor darling working so late. Come and sit down and relax before supper.'

Hardly was I seated before one daughter brought me my slippers and propped my feet on a foot stool, and the other had poured me a cold beer.

Husbands, fathers of daughters, or any fathers for that matter will know that behaviour of this kind is so abnormal as to be positively frightening. I ceased to relax and demanded and explanation.

All fled to the kitchen from whence came agitated twitterings.

Presently all three emerged and lined up sheepishly before me. Eldest daughter then produced from behind her back the latest applicant for family membership. It had been scrubbed and disinfected from nose to tail and for one of the few times in its life was sparkling white.

Dogs are not stupid, it knew immediately that this was the final and fatal interview. It cringed flat on the floor at my feet, gazed imploringly up at me with soft brown eyes and wagged its tail hopefully.

The word flood broke. Jumbled phrases tumbled together.

"Poor little dog – isn't it sweet – no home- starving to death – always beaten"

I prefer bending with the wind to ignominious rout and as a reward I was allowed to name it. I called him 'Whitefang' in protest. It was the most totally unsuitable name that I could think of.

For years variously assorted dogs ranging from a neurotic white Alsatian to a kind of fox terrier with a passion for low life, passed through the house and in due course went the way of all flesh.

My two beautiful Alsatians, Zeus and Molly, whom I had had from puppies and who predated my marriage, succumbed to old age. Alex went nursing and Sarah to boarding school, and suddenly the house was empty except for one cat and Fang, then Fang was also gone.

Fang (mercifully shortened since he was seldom white) was one of the only four men I have known in my life whom I would have classified as lady killers. None, including Fang, were either particularly good looking, charming or even intelligent.

They did have one thing in common and that was the extraordinary belief that no woman would ever say 'No' to them.

Few did.

Fang despite his diminutive size was convinced that he was what every bitch on heat was looking for. They responded to this huge ego with enthusiasm and to the discomfort of other suitors.

Great Danes, Alsatians, Dobermans, Rotweilers, Labradors all fell under the spell and suffered the resulting unrequited love arising from a ground clearance difference of two feet.

We were living in Kariba in Northern Zimbabwe at the time. The town is sited on hills overlooking the huge lake created for a hydro-electric scheme. When it was built in 1955 it was the largest man made lake in the world, it is also the centre of a large wildlife area and residents have to co-exist with a certain amount of game.

On the fatal evening Fang escaped from our yard and visited a Labrador bitch which was particularly besotted with him, he dallied too long and returning after dusk met not an irate husband, but a hungry leopard on the Post office steps – a fate witnessed by a number of passers by.

At least it must have been a mercifully brief end for an aging lady killer, returning home from another illegal assignation. There were probably worse ways to go.

Talking of wildlife, apart from leopards the biggest nuisances were baboons and elephants. Baboons will occur later, elephants though could be a real nuisance. We had one once in the garden standing nine feet from us and pulling Jean's pot plants out from under the veranda roof whilst we shouted imprecations from the safety of the front door. They love clean water and a swimming pool is an open invitation for a drink. One problem being that they also flatten your front gate and fence when accessing this oasis. Oddly enough they hate being sprayed with a hosepipe and will leave at a run. This, I have to say, was, at that time, an interesting way to get rid of them as the water pressure was usually low to say the least.

However, my favourite elephant story concerned a middle aged lady who had just moved up to Kariba. As I said it is built on hills and the road up is narrow and winding cut out of the hillside. Driving home one evening she came round a corner to find three elephants occupying the centre of the road. She was on her own and very nervous, behind her was a sharp curve which (being female) she did not want to try and reverse round, on the other hand she could not go forward. She wound up her front windows and sat gripping the steering wheel and praying for them to move.

Then she felt the tiniest whisper of something moving her hair at the back of her neck. Petrified she looked in her mirrors - she had forgotten to close the rear window, and an elephant stood by the car with its trunk through this gently sniffing her hair with its trunk!

As with anyone possessed of passable hearing, eyesight and the ability to look around me, I prefer dogs to people, but to truly enjoy the best of a dog you need to get it as a puppy and raise it yourself. Jean had never had a puppy in her life.

I decided that the time had come, but puppies like children are a long term commitment, one which should never be undertaken lightly. I like to take my dogs with me whenever I can. In this respect big dogs are a problem. In any case I always hate seeing big dogs confined to small spaces.

I read once that miniature dachshunds are the preferred dogs for ageing bourgeois, also I have to admit that my mother had had two. Well I was an ageing bourgeois! I phoned a kennel in Harare three hundred miles away – I was looking for a smooth haired miniature dachshund bitch – a puppy, did they know of anyone selling any?

I know more about the vagaries of fate than anyone else, but some things are fated. They told me that someone had had a litter a few days previously and gave me his phone number. I phoned and found I was talking to our dentist. He had a bitch, smooth haired and black and tan.

I didn't tell Jean.

Eight weeks later we were sitting having an evening drink on the club veranda when I saw the five year old son of a friend, Ryan Moan, coming carefully towards me. They had just returned from a trip to Harare.

He held his cupped hands out in front of him with enormous concentration and in their centre was a black hole. So tiny that she fitted comfortably inside a five year old's hands, and so black, black, pitch black that she didn't appear to have any form at all.

Then when I took her from him I saw that each minute leg ended in a tan paw and the sides and bottom of her muzzle were tan. Her eyes were as black and shiny as her coat and above each was a tiny tan dash of an eyebrow.

I gave her to Jean.

She terrified us she was so minute and frail.

The young are optimists, the older you get the more frequently you have observed Murphy's Law in action and the more you anticipate it being applied to you.

Unless you work in a nursing home you also tend to forget the responsibility of looking after new things. I had just had this demonstrated to me. I had spent a night in Harare with friends.

"Would I mind baby sitting for a couple of hours?" they asked because it was their night for a dancing class.

Naturally I said I would be delighted, I had raised two daughters and was an expert on small babies, even two month old ones. We had dinner and they departed.

After half an hour it seemed t me that the house was ominously quiet. Things like cot deaths (which I had never given a thought to with my children) sprang to mind. I went through to the nursery and had a look. The room was dim and I didn't want to switch on the light and wake it – but was it breathing?

I knelt next to the cot and listened, peered at it through the cot bars and still couldn't make up my mind. I began rehearsing what one might say to parents who went off and left you with an alive baby and came back to find you with a dead one!

Finally I poked it gently with my finger and thank heaven, it twitched of its own accord. I spent the next two hours poking it every ten minutes to make sure.

We felt the same way about our newest acquisition, she was so small, would she really keep on breathing? What terrible traumas had been caused by her forcible removal from her parents and siblings and a four hour car journey – her first.

We needn't have worried.

There are people who know from their first breath that the world was created especially for them. All new things, smells, sights, and feelings are there to delight and not affright – she was one. She was not the slightest bit perturbed, only interested.

We worried that night that she would be lonely and miserable and cry, so after some discussion we decided to put her between us in the double bed.

After half an hour I felt a series of tiny, but forceful rabbit kicks on my back. Her ladyship considered that we were lying a little too close together and required more room! The only people who didn't sleep that night were Jean and I. We were petrified that we would roll over and crush her.

The next morning the struggle for a name began.

Naming children you have to consider the children. William Charles and Lance Oswald Omerigood are almost certainly doomed to miserable schooldays. Naming dogs you have to consider yourself, to their subsequent regret, many owners fail to give adequate attention to this aspect.

As far as I am aware dogs are indifferent to their names, that is to say, I have never observed even the most misnamed dogs cringe in company when their names were called.

It can be otherwise with owners, and we had two recent examples to remind us.

Fang was the first, having given him an unsuitable name we were stuck with it.

'FANG, FANG' you would call, and this small dirty white ball of fluff would come fawning to your feet. Then if you looked around you would find nearby strangers rolling their eyes nervously in every direction as they waited for some huge savage Doberman or the like, to come pounding up in answer to the call.

The other one was a weakness on my part and had taken up residence whist we were waiting for our puppy. She was a large boxer cross bitch with a very sweet nature who had belonged to a friend of mine. He had gone on leave and asked us to keep an eye on the dog which was staying at the house and would be looked after by his domestic servant.

I went down on a few evenings to make sure she was being fed, then on the fifth day she turned up at our house.

I took her back.

She came back.

Feeling responsible, we took her in and became fond of her. She was an excellent guard dog and it was immediately after Zimbabwe's independence at a time when as the Police and legal system degenerated, crime, including burglaries was showing the inevitable increase.

When Jon returned, I explained the position and asked if he was interested in parting with her. He was only too happy as it turned out that she had actually belonged to his wife who had recently left him.

Up to this time we didn't know her name, so I asked.

"Spot or Damnit" he replied

I queried these rather unsatisfactory alternatives.

"Well" he said "all dogs are called Spot as far as I'm concerned and Damnit – well Damnit"

I refused point blank to have a dog called Spot, especially when she was a nice even tan colour all over. Of course we could have changed her name, but she did answer to Damnit, so Damnit she stayed.

It seemed a bit of a joke at the time, and it wasn't long before you would call her by name without thinking about it at all.

Try standing in the middle of a crowded street shouting "DAMNIT DAMNIT" at the top of your voice and see the looks you get! I was determined that our latest acquisition shouldn't suffer and that neither should we.

Arguments raged for three days. I read once that dachshunds are in fact believed to have originated from Egypt, but to modern minds they are definitely Germanic dogs. It turned out that we knew practically no German girls' names.

Helga sounded vaguely deutcher but didn't have the right ring at all. I started with Fritz and ended with Fritzella but Jean didn't like it, and I can't say I was happy about it either.

By tortuous paths whose meanderings I can't recall, Fritzella became Fenella. This sounded nice, seemed harmless and met none of our original criteria, so it stuck.

The abbreviation 'Fen' was also harmless.

For some reason unknown to me all our girls acquire the second name of Jane, whether they were christened with it or not, so Fenella Jane Lousada she became.

She was a delight.

She was also, miracle of miracles, housetrained by our dentist before we got her, the only puppy I have ever had which was. Whilst the size of her offerings was not such as to cause much tribulation, it did mean that her life with us started without the first painful disciplining.

I got her for Jean, but a variety of circumstances, and no doubt considerable selfishness on my part, finally made her very much my dog.

One of the reasons was that Jean was working in a shop during the mornings and couldn't take her, whereas I had a job which enabled me keep her with me at all times.

The other was that Jean was terrified that if she took her out some larger animal would eat her, or she would get dropped, or fall off a cliff, or be struck by lightning, or run over, or snatched by an eagle or …

I was careful but I never worried too much about her.

From the day we got her and for all her life so far, the world has fascinated her. She loves new places, new smells, and new sights. They are all put there for her to investigate.

Her first taste of discipline came with the car. In the beginning she was so small that her behaviour made no difference, but as she grew bigger and tried to climb all over me as I drove, it was necessary to rebuff her.

There were occasions when it was convenient to leave her in the car for short periods. This met with dissent, but she learnt remarkably quickly, although like all dachsies her obedience levels were governed largely by her appreciation of the situation and her desires not yours.

She also learnt very quickly for herself.

In Africa longish car journeys are the norm, and she could soon distinguish between long and short ones.

On a short journey you would soon be arriving somewhere new so it was worth staying alert and awake and watching what was going on. A long journey could be boring, so as soon as she as sure that we were set for one she would settle down beside me on the bench seat and go to sleep.

Any change though, would wake her instantly. Sound the horn, brake sharply, change gears and she would be up immediately to see what was going on.

If driving slowly her favourite position is standing on my lap with her front paws on my right arm and her head out of the window, (Zimbabwe did not have English driving laws)

Fen has long silky ears, when she runs they fly out sideways like butterfly wings, but with her head out of the car window they streamed behind her. So closely does she resemble A.E. Shepherd's drawing of Piglet in a high wind that it is impossible not to feel that she must have modelled for him in a previous existence.

Once we went faster the wind would become too much and she would demand to get on my shoulders. We owned a pick-up at the time and she fitted comfortably across the top of the seat behind me, jammed between the window and the back of my neck. This gave her an excellent view out.

Most dogs like to look out of cars when they are travelling but she is the only one I have ever seen who tried to look round corners as you approached them. You see people do it, they instinctively cock their heads slightly to one side to peer round. Fen did exactly the same.

She has travelled hundreds of thousands of miles in cars and generally is as good as gold. Only when she is bored with sleeping will she demand to get on someone's lap so she can have a look at what's going on.

Her only other problem is that naturally she expects to travel in the front seat.

Fenella, from birth, has had a firm view of her place in the world hierarchy – and that is at the top.

This arises not (as in people's cases) from delusions of grandeur, selfishness or oriental desire for face, but purely from that inborn knowledge which allows royalty to refer to itself as 'we'.

It's fairly common to hear people say of their dogs that the dogs think they are human. This has always seemed to me to be a rather egotistical outlook, in Fen's case there is no doubt what she thinks.

Fenella, I am certain, knows perfectly well that she is a dachshund, she would never condescend to be 'a people'! The only thing is that I am equally convinced that she is just as sure that Jean and I are also dachshunds of a rather deformed and overgrown breed. In her heart she probably pities our deformities.

She has only one psychological scar and that is cats.

As Kipling says all proper dogs chase cats, but there is chasing cats and chasing cats, so to speak. Fenella has an obsession about them. It arose like this.

We usually had the odd cat around the house and immediately prior to Fen's arrival we had a pink one. I think there is a particular name for that colour, but pink is the closest I can get. It was an amiable very domesticated and harmless cat and used to sleep on the end of the bed by my feet.

Nearby at the Country Sports Club, a number of wild cats flourished, garnishing scraps from the kitchen and hunting for a living.

I was jerked awake in the early hours of one morning by the sounds of a cat fight which appeared to be taking place in the passage from our bedroom to the front door. Because of the heat we slept with all the doors and windows open, and usually naked. I leapt out of bed and stormed down the passage making suitable roaring sounds of displeasure.

In the dimness I half saw, half sensed, a cat flee out through the front door, I returned satisfied to bed. Shortly afterwards I felt the cat jump back on the bed and settle by my feet.

I am seldom at my best in the early mornings, so when I woke up, opened a bleary eye and viewed my feet, I thought for a moment that the demon drink had finally caught up with me.

Only it was neither pink elephant nor pink cat that I saw. Lying on the end of the bed lay a new cat – grey with the black rings of its wildcat ancestry.

She was in appalling condition, had milk fever and was starving. Whether she had once belonged to someone and been abandoned, or whether she had always been wild we will never know. Nor oddly enough was she the first or last cat who walked into our houses and took up residence. She obviously belonged to the collection of club cats. It was the rainy season and it seemed likely that she had had kittens and these had either been taken by a bigger predator or washed away by a storm and drowned.

Whatever the circumstances she had decided that domestication was the only hope and had come to throw herself on our mercy. Fortunately the vet was in town that day on his monthly visit, so she was disinfected, treated for various diseases and spayed all in one traumatic morning. Having come to us of her own free will she made no objection to being handled although it was likely that she had never been touched by a human before.

Thereafter she stayed some years until she finally disappeared one night, presumably a prey to a larger predator.

She was from the start totally domesticated except for her hunting. Having done this for a living she never gave it up even when it was no longer necessary. In some ways it was a blessing and in some a nuisance.

Jean loves birds and we had plenty in the garden. We also had a bird bath standing about three feet high. She would lie some fifteen feet away watching this until a bird came down, then galvanised into action run, leap in the air and catch it as it took off. We reached a point where we actively discouraged birds.

On the other hand she was a great snake killer and Kariba had snakes to spare though one seldom saw them. This was always a worry, more for the dogs than for us, as boomslangs and mambas, two of the most poisonous in the world were common, not to mention the more mundane cobras and puff adders.

She caught at least three a week which we felt must be keeping the population in the garden down and was a small price for her habit of consuming them on the lounge carpet.

Shortly after this and before Fen's arrival pink cat disappeared.

Keeping animals in Kariba was not always satisfactory. You had to keep dogs in from dusk to dawn and even then you had to be careful. A friend jogging along the main road at five one evening, his Labrador trotting five yards behind him, had it taken by a leopard.

Although the main leopard diet was baboons, dogs to leopards are as caviar and vodka are to Russians.

Another friend was sitting in his lounge one evening when a leopard chased his dog straight through, past him and into the kitchen. Fortunately it then realised it was out of place and left without causing any more fuss, pursued by my friend trying to hit it with a chair – his only weapon!

We brought Fen home that first evening and put her on the couch, she was the approximate size of two match boxes laid end to end.

A few minutes later in came cat (somehow or other she never got a name) took one look at this minute patch of black and retired slowly hissing and spitting with all her fur on end.

Goodness knows what she thought it was. I was prepared for her to try and eat her, after all I reasoned that to a hunting cat Fen would have looked like a tasty morsel. Not at all, Fen was so alien that she never came to terms with her presence and hated her, from day one.

Neither was it a pacific hate. She must have soon realised that killing Fen was unacceptable, but anything short of this was. Fenella, as soon as she came across cat for the first time, investigated her in a friendly way with play in mind. A sharp tap across the nose with unsheathed claws soon disillusioned her.

But cat was never content to merely fend off advances. She took to waiting round the corners of furniture in hunting stances. When Fen trotted unsuspectingly round she would receive a quick left and right to the head before cat fled.

The attacks were completely unprovoked and I can't recall that Fen ever showed the slightest desire to attack cat. It would have been futile anyway as she was only about a tenth of the size.

These early memories became burnt into her mind in the best Freudian style – they have never left her. Since most cats are as big as she is even now, they are approached with caution at close range, but let them run and she will give full blooded chase becoming quite hysterical in the process. Its not that she doesn't like cats, she loathes and detests cats with a passionate hatred that I doubt even old age will temper or eradicate.

To be honest I am not that enamoured of cats myself and one benefit is that we have never been able to own another one as any effort to bring a kitten into the house would certainly lead to its instant demise.

When Fenella was about four months old I taught her to swim.

Kariba, (if you can bear the heat) is not only unique among lakes but is one of the most beautiful ones you will ever come across. Its hallmark is the forests of petrified trees in the water near the shoreline. These are one of the finest examples of Murphy's Law that you will ever come across.

Put a wooden boat on the lake and within six months it is so riddled with dry rot that you can throw it away. Put a tree in the water where you don't want it and thirty years later despite, water, heat, humidity and the attentions of numerous borer type beetles, it is not only still there but as hard as rock.

The lake is surrounded by untouched bush and wild life area and the shoreline is indented with hundreds of small bays and river mouths. It has some of the most magnificent sunsets and sunrises you will ever see, it is truly beautiful.

There is always a price, in Kariba it is the heat, often into the 40 Celsius range and the care you have to take of crocodiles.

I owned in succession a number of sailing boats ranging from an aged 505 racing dinghy to a thirty foot long keel cruiser. Whenever possible I spent at least five days a month on the lake, and had no intention of leaving Fenella behind. She would make tempting croc bait so where she swam would have to be carefully monitored, but it was necessary that she could in case she fell overboard.

I started her on the yacht club slipway, calling her to come to me whilst I stood ankle deep in the water. Each time she reached me I made a great fuss over her and then moved a little further out. The water was about the same temperature as the air so there was no danger of her catching cold.

In retrospect the effort I put into these lessons was completely wasted. Fenella is one of the arguments for re-incarnation, in a previous life she must have been an otter.

She loved water.

She not only swam well but fast and enjoyed it. People were always rescuing her from pools. " Poor little thing" they said "she must be getting so tired."

Playing with children I have seen her stay in the water without a break for fifty minutes, she is amazingly quick, tail wagging furiously the whole time.

I once considered having her tail operated on to make it flat like a beavers I thought it would give her at least an extra knot or two in speed. Regrettably none of the veterinary surgeons I knew would admit to having mastered the technique required for this operation.

Like most dachsies Fen is very much a one person dog. She is not fond of being fondled by strangers, nor will she go to them. Swimmers are the exception, anyone swimming is a friend and a potential playmate.

Her favourite game is to swim up to you and you are meant to dive and try and escape underwater. I have seen her put her head underwater to look, but generally in clear water she can watch you from the surface. When you emerge she is waiting.

This can be remarkably exhausting and with children she has to be watched carefully. She gets overexcited and grabs a mouthful of your hair as you come up, giving it a sharp tug. This can be painful – and it is nearly impossible to out swim her underwater. After a time you begin to feel like a submarine with an enemy destroyer on the surface above you.

Even fully-grown she only weighs about ten pounds and you would think that it would be easy to push something that small away from you as you surfaced.

It isn't. A push was considered part of the game and she redoubles her efforts to get at you which means that unless you are very careful you get badly scratched by the wind milling paws.

It is always easy to see when she is getting tired. At first she swims horizontally, then as time passes her rear end begins to sink until the wagging tail is no longer visible. Finally she swims perpendicularly with only her head out of the water, like a person treading water.

But she never knew when she had had enough and complained loudly and vociferously when removed. If there were still swimmers in the water she would wriggle and wraggle and struggle fiercely to get away from you.

It is not my habit to admit that Fenella has any imperfections. I once took her to a vet who gave her a once over and then muttered something about 'she's got a bit of an under slung jaw, hasn't she?'

My experience of vets has always been that they are the nicest class of people (not to mention the most expensive) in the world. I find this unsurprising presumably they became vets because they like animals better than the human race. To me this alone is enough to explain why they have such nice natures.

Regrettably in every profession there will always be at least one incompetent fool. Naturally that was the last Lousada business that particular man received.

But she does have one unpleasing habit and that is her hunting shriek.

With age it has become slightly muted, but when she was young it was unbearable. I say shriek because that was what it was, not a yelp or a howl or a bark – a shriek. Very high pitched, almost continuous and of extraordinary volume and carrying power.

I doubt whether in days of yore when the rack performed its gruesome tasks the victims can have made such noises.

Dachsies are hounds and great hunting dogs (although suitable sized prey is not readily come by) and when in full flight after something, particularly a cat, out came this ghastly noise. How she found breath to make it I have no idea.

When she was over excited, hysterical, tired or denied her way she also gave tongue in a similar vein.

If she was swimming with me she could keep up with my breaststroke, but not once I changed to crawl. She would follow at full pace giving hunting screams.

I tried to avoid giving her cause, but there were occasions when I had to persuade strangers that there was no need to call the RSPCA – IMMEDIATELY.

Age and possibly passive pipe smoking, have lowered the pitch and reduced the volume until nowadays it is almost endurable. Age and maturity have also tempered her behaviour so that she no longer becomes hysterical with too much excitement.

Her swimming gave rise to one other talent which fascinated onlookers – her racing dive.

There are lots of dogs and breeds of dogs which love water and will jump in at the drop of a swimming costume, but I have never seen another that could do a racing dive. Hold her ten yards from the water's edge, have someone call her and let her go. Off she will go flat out and dive in – front legs extended horizontally in front and back legs stretched out straight behind, and all four paws perfectly pointed.

I have a marvellous photo of her caught in mid air doing it. The only slight blemish is the tail which instead of also being extended straight, tends to curl up at an angle.

I began taking her with me on the boat. She was never worried about being surrounded by water and was remarkably well behaved. I had worried that she would jump off at inopportune moments, especially as I usually sailed single handed.

She never did, somehow she knew that it wasn't done – she didn't have to be taught. If I got in the water then she was in like a flash and once we were moored ashore she might have a swim from the shore if she felt like it, but she never jumped off if we were moving.

Boats provided one of her first close calls with disaster.

The Christmas after her first birthday (Fenella's) we gave Sarah a windsurfer.

I am a becomingly modest man, but I hold the strong belief that I am capable of competently managing any vessel which is wind propelled.

Sarah being young was soon master of her board, with me it was otherwise. This was not due to any particular difference in ability or capability, but was in my view, a simple result of the laws of gravity.

Not only was I taller than Sarah and considerably heavier, but my centre of gravity, situated regrettably in my middle was also higher. All this meant that it was much harder for me to keep the silly thing upright.

The first morning I tried to master it I got an ear infection from spending so much time submerged. Finally the board and I called it a draw. In calm weather with a steady breeze I was master, in any other situations it was. I felt that honour was satisfied and have never been near one since.

Fenella loved the board. It was exciting to sit on, fun, watery and generally an ideal plaything for a dachsie. When I was learning it was exceptionally exciting and watery!

It was impossible to leave her ashore as any efforts by Jean or the children to constrain her resulted in hysterical shrieks.

On one occasion when the board and I parted company especially violently, I came to the surface and looked for her. She was nowhere in sight.

The board was a little distance away with the sail floating on the far side of it. Assuming that she was hidden from me by the board, I swum over and climbed back on, stood up and looked around – no Fenella.

I began to panic, then my eye was caught by a movement in the sail. As I looked a piece in the middle formed itself in to a point and rose up momentarily from the water. The sail flattened out and then it happened again.

She had got caught underneath and was coming up vertically trying to push her nose through it. A frantic dive and I had rescued her. It didn't put her off or upset her at all. Once she had blown the water out of her nose and shaken it out of her ears and eyes she was perfectly ready to continue.

The wind surfer did bring to light one of her few blind spots.

I have never known her lost – take her to a place once and she will remember it always. She could differentiate immediately between the sound of our car, and even the sound of our car door shutting, and any other vehicle, but boats were different.

Just as anyone who was swimming was a friend, so I think she must view boats. All boats are boats are boats. Size, shape, type is a matter of indifference, if it's a boat it must be OUR boat...

This also applied to windsurfers, of which there were quite a few at the yacht club. She was so good at recognising things and knowing what was what, that this had never occurred to me.

We were sitting in the club house sited some fifty feet above the lake, when someone said 'Isn't that Fenella'

I looked. A hundred yards out and heading towards the horizon was the tiny dot of a black head. I yelled at the top of my lungs until finally she heard me, realised where I was, and turned and swam back.

Then beyond her I saw the reason, a windsurfer was being sailed further out on the bay, she had seen it from the clubhouse, immediately assumed it was ours and headed.

From then on I had to keep a careful watch on her otherwise she took off after any one she saw. Nor does she forget. She didn't see one subsequently for over eight years, then anchored one day in the Greek islands two girls came paddling past on a board. She leapt off the boat into our dinghy, out of the dinghy onto the board and became hysterical when she wasn't allowed to go off on it.

She also had to be watched with boats. If she was actually with me there was no problem, but if I wasn't and she saw a boat leaving, a ghastly feeling would seize her that I had abandoned her and gone off on that boat – WITHOUT HER.

Into the water she would go after it.

Over the years she has improved slightly but still experiences difficulty.

In a crowded marina she will go to the right pontoon but is likely to stand waiting hopefully by the side of any boat in the rough area of ours.

For a seafaring dog I have to admit that I find this behaviour a little embarrassing.

She and Jean have a lot in common, Jean had the same problem with cars. When we were first married I owned a white VW Beetle. We would park it in town, arrange to meet back at the car and separate to go shopping.

I would arrive and wait and wait.

At last I caught on – it wasn't simple feminine tardiness. If Jean wasn't there it was only necessary to walk a little way up or down the street. White Beetles were a dime a dozen in those days and I would invariably find her standing patiently next to someone else's.

Jean was as besotted with Fenella as I was.

'But' she said 'shouldn't we find a husband for her so she won't be lonely?'

Chapter Two

"Buy a puppy and your money will buy
Love unflinching that cannot lie
Perfect passion and worship fed
By a kick in the ribs or a pat on the head
Nevertheless it is hardly fair
To risk your heart for a dog to tear'.

R. Kipling

I objected most strongly, we had our puppy and now she was nearly full grown.

Some time" Jean said "we will almost certainly have to put her into kennels for a short period at least. If we had two they would be much happier."

I held out whilst water dripped on the stone, but she did have a point. We planned to go to England the following year to see my parents and would be away nearly two months. She could not come as she would have to go into quarantine (there were no pets passports or microchips in those days), so she would have to stay in kennels because leaving her with friends would place too big a responsibility on their shoulders.

There was another factor.

I'm sure that it is no hardship and possibly even an advantage for a bitch to be spayed without having had puppies; nonetheless I always have this sneaking feeling that biological cause and effect need to be given a chance.

Men are apparently made so that they can kill each other, women so that they can make replacement men and bitches so that they can have puppies.

I didn't want puppies. I knew they would be an invitation to emotional disaster. I was not, no matter what pressure was brought to bear on me, going to keep any of them. This meant that the departure of each to its new home would be accompanied by tears and matrimonial recriminations – not to mention my feelings.

Yet if Fenella was to have as full a life as possible shouldn't she have the chance to be a mother – not to mention some sexual experience?

Like so many good intentions this view tended to centre on what I thought, and not what Fenella thought. On the other hand despite generally excellent communications there was no way that I could actually ascertain her opinion on such a complicated matter.

Had I done so, I fancy in retrospect, that her vote would have been a firm and unequivocal 'NO'.

I weakened slowly and eventually the inevitable happened and I gave in.

"Alright" I said "let's keep and eye out for a suitable male puppy. If we can find one, we can *consider it*" *All husbands will* recognise that statements of this nature are tantamount to total capitulation.

Miniature dachshunds are not that common in Zimbabwe. Jean scanned the papers and phoned kennels without any joy. We heard of nothing for over a month and I was beginning to reconsider when Jean found an advertisement in the paper.

We phoned them – they had a male puppy and owned both parents, however they had inherited these from friends leaving the country and had no papers for them or knowledge of their ancestry.

I am not a pedigree man, I have had highly pedigreed dogs, but for every one we must have owned five mongrels. This was different, if he was to be a mate for Fenella he must be pure bred and small.

It was not so much that this would effect the sale of the puppies (although this was a consideration) as if there was a large ancestor in his background or he himself grew too big, then the puppies might be too large and cause Fenella problems at birth.

As a result I was loath to consider a puppy of unknown ancestry. Jean of course wanted him sight unseen. We had already been looking for some time with no success, if we didn't find one soon we would be unable to take it anyway because it would be too young to leave behind when we went to Europe.

I phoned my dentist. Please could someone go and have a look as the puppies were in Harare. He phoned the Chairperson of the dachshund club, very kindly she went round and had a look.

"The parents looked alright" she said "they weren't too large and had good heads".

We phoned booked the smallest dog and in late February 1985 Jean, I and Fenella drove through to fetch him. We never found out his exact birthday, but then he is Jean's dog and she can never remember mine, so I don't suppose he minds too much.

We found a bungalow set in a walled garden and what the owners told us was the perfect security set up for the uncontrolled crime wave, two miniature dachshunds and two Dobermans.

'The dachsies wake the Dobermans' they said 'and the Dobermans put paid to the intruders'.

The parents didn't impress me much, but then both were tan and I had Fenella with me. Naturally comparisons of other dogs against Fenella tend to show the others in a poor light. However, at least they looked reasonable.

Our puppy was a golden tan all over and Jean adored him on sight.

We paid, Jean put him on her lap wrapped in a towel and I got in the car with Fenella. Fenella took a look, and then a closer look, and, in a polite way she expressed her displeasure.

"Other dogs" she said "were not really her thing. No doubt they were acceptable in their own place, but what was this apology for an animal doing in OUR car?" That was certainly not the right place.

I calmed her down and settled her on the bench seat beside me whilst Jean cooed over our latest acquisition.

He had huge liquid golden eyes almost the colour of his coat, and these looked out apprehensively on a strange world, not to mention the strange black dog a few inches away from him. The engine noise, despite the Japanese maker's best efforts, also unsettled him as did the peculiar motion.

We had a four hour drive ahead of us and so it seemed a suitable time to consider a name. In fact it took about ten minutes and we were in perfect agreement. If ever there had been a desert rat, he was it.

Well you simply couldn't call a dog Montgomery' could you? Anyway dachshunds are meant to be German – so Rommel Lousada he became.

It has not proved a totally apt name.

Whilst in some ways he has fulfilled his namesake's attacking genius, I do not recall that the Field Marshal himself was a mass of Freudian neuroses. Also Rommel (the General) did discriminate as to whom he attacked. Our Rommel turned out to have no such scruples.

At the time though, these experiences were all in the future, all we had was a very pretty (handsome?), very nervous, very tiny puppy.

From the beginning Rommel was the antithesis of Fenella in every way. His huge brown eyes had a ring of white round them when they were fully open. When he rolled them apprehensively at a wide hostile world he managed to convey an impression of absolute terror at his surroundings.

To Rommel, the sky when blue is something that unless watched carefully may fall on you at any moment. If you re a small dachsie this is an alarming thought – there is a lot of sky to fall! Cloudy skies merely serve to conceal unimagined large predatory animals, all having evil designs on small dogs.

Rain is a nerve wracking experience, who knew what it was or where it came from, it also appeared to be made up one hundred percent of his non-favourite element – water. In exculpation it must be said that rain was something of a rarity at that time and he was almost a year old before he saw his first.

Then there was thunder.

Damnit was terrified of thunder and at the first sound would flee into the house and remain buried under the dining room table quivering with nerves until long after it had passed.

Whether her example affected Rommel I have no way of knowing, but I doubt it. Personally I believe he has a guilty conscience.

To Rommel, thunder was retribution with a capital 'R'. It was beyond any doubt a great dog of unparalleled ferocity and unimaginable size that lurked in the sky and was after ROMMEL!

For Rommel, right from the start, suffered under an unfortunate misapprehension. This was that he was in the dog world the counterpart of an upgraded combination of Sylvester Stallone and Arnold Schwarzenegger.

Most puppies tend to bark at other dogs when they are young and before they have learnt discretion. In the majority of cases they are ignored or sniffed over and soon learn that it safer to be polite to your biggers.

Unfortunately in Rommel's case all the dogs he barked at immediately fled, pursued by Rommel, at the maximum pace that two inch long legs would carry him.

Many years ago my parents owned a large Alsatian named Groucho after his eyebrows. He was a terrible fighter and would attack any other dog he saw unless it immediately indicated its subservience by rolling on its back or running away.

We lived in central Tanganyika at the time and owned an open back pickup truck. I recall one day visiting a store where the owner, a Greek, had a Pekinese. Pekes have, of course, very poor eyesight and a poor sense of smell and hearing, on top of this they have been raised for years on the myth that they are Chinese lion hunting dogs – although as far as I know there are no lions in China.

I owned one once and a study revealed that its field of vision was about six feet. Every time a door swung open with a gust of wind it would attack it. It never learnt and did neither its teeth nor its nose much good, although since its nose was already squashed flat further damage to this appendage was invisible. If something moved it was alive – if it was alive and near you attack it. It was a simple philosophy of life.

I might add it also had no sense of direction and was a great wanderer. We lived in a very small community in the centre of a very wild tribal trust land in Zimbabwe. The locals, fortunately, had never seen a dog like this before so at least it was easily recognisable. If it became bored it revolved slowly five or six times like a wayward compass and then set off in a straight line in the direction it was pointing. It either couldn't or wouldn't be bothered to find its way back, and when tired simply awaited rescue. It was found (and kindly returned to me) one day from five kilometres away where it had been happily trotting along behind a hunter among his pack of hunting dogs.

Anyway the Greek's peke had the same attacking philosophy. The car stopped, Groucho jumped off the back, the peke emerged from the store and attacked.

Groucho who, faced with a Doberman, bull terrier or any other dog would have instantaneously tried to slaughter them, leapt back into the truck. From its safety he peered nervously down over the side at this peculiar visitation making unidentifiable squeaking noises.

For ten minutes the peke circled the truck getting more and more hysterical with frustration at its inability to jump high enough to reach him. Groucho circled round inside looking down. No power on earth would get him out.

The fact was that he had no idea what it was. It didn't resemble any dog he had ever seen nor did it sound much like one. Whilst it was undoubtedly very small its ferociousness indicated that perhaps it had a hidden weapon of great potency. In the circumstances caution was the order of the day.

Dogs faced with Rommel felt exactly the same way. They simply didn't know what this walking miniature sausage was – and they ran.

This regrettably led early in his life to the unalterable conviction that all other dogs were afraid of him. It took many years for a modicum of sense to enter his head and it causes us many problems. It is also a miracle that he has survived without being seriously bitten by a larger dog.

Planarian worms have been taught to respond to multi-choice questions in laboratories, Bosnians and Serbs finally learnt there was some logic and reason in peace, elephants have long memories and sound reasoning processes.

Fenella can, within limitations, reason, she can draw inferences and she can communicate her wants, watch her carefully and you can usually see the way her mind works.

With Rommel it was otherwise from the beginning. No-on can follow his convoluted thought processes. He closes his eyes to slits giving him a Mongolian look, then deep inside some prehistoric cortex a series of uncontrolled connections take place and a thought is born.

This rare occurrence follows no known law of dog logic and I often think takes place quite independently of Rommel's own volition. It makes him a difficult dog to communicate with.

Aside from killing other dogs it soon transpired that he had one other grand passion in life and that was food.

Fen is a picky eater. Her favourite food is chicken, preferably raw, but cooked will do. Put one pea in her food and it will be carefully nosed out and finally left sitting in solitary splendour in the centre of an empty plate. She is not a vegetarian!

If we are eating something she becomes more enthusiastic. Doubtless this belief originates in the not totally unfounded reasoning that we probably keep the better things for ourselves. But even then such unacceptable dachshund foods as vegetables won't be taken.

The only guaranteed method of getting her to eat something she doesn't fancy, is to put it in my mouth first. Fortunately she is seldom ill, but when she is and needs to eat, it guarantees her top class fare. I draw the line at masticating pieces of unidentifiable dog's food before feeding them to her. Chicken (cooked) I am prepared to suffer.

She also has an infuriating habit of rejecting food, either when she isn't hungry or doesn't approve of it. She puts her nose under one side of the dish and flips it upside down emptying the contents onto the floor. Then she will stroll away with an air that says quite plainly "Don't try passing that muck off on me again."

Rommel on the other hand will eat anything – meat, peas, cabbage, grapes, oranges, apples and anything suitably smelly and rotten that he can find lying around. What's more he will eat and eat whether he is hungry or not.

Dachsies don't usually have large litters and I never found out how many brothers and sisters he had, but we can only assume that he was seventh puppy and suffered from nipple deprivation syndrome when a baby. That at least would be the modern interpretation, myself I think its just pure greed.

One result was that he grew apace in all four directions.

Mostly it is muscle. Rommel will never suffer from that scourge of dachshunds – slipped discs. Other dachsies may be long and supple, not Rommel. Pick him up by either end and the other sticks straight out – his middle is too solid to bend.

His weight also precluded him from taking part in swimming activities. As soon as he was big enough we endeavoured to teach him, it was not a success. Water was not an element that appealed to Rommel. It was wet, it was unpredictable – little waves went up your nose, it wasn't firm enough to be walked on and it didn't seem to have any bottom.

Simply it was not his thing, in a bowl where it behaved itself and could be drunk it was acceptable, in large quantities definitely not.

He did try – and he can swim – just. His specific centre of gravity is too high or too low (I never, even at school, knew which was which), there is just too much solid Rommel and too much thin water. Rommel tends to sink and he has too few and too small legs to provide adequate lift and propulsion.

If Jean and I both go in the water he will swim to us, but having reached us and duty done the shore beckons and back he goes.

We long ago stopped trying to make him. The whole process is too transparently painful and nerve wracking. He swims with his head just above the water and with eyes tightly closed to tiny slits so that he sees as little water as is compatible with maintaining direction.

Not unnaturally he views boats with the same misgiving. He is happy enough to get on board and whilst the boat is attached to the shore suffers no alarm, but once he is out 'there' surrounded by that terrible substance he has one idea and one idea only. That is to keep the best lookout possible for land and once it is sighted never to take his eyes off it lest it disappear again.

Jean and he are kindred spirits. When in a boat Jean likes to have land firmly in view and spends most of her time computing whether it is close enough for her and Rommel to swim to if the boat sinks. Rommel thinks the same.

The second the bows ground he is off onto a solid element with a sigh of relief and not a backward glance. Sailing parallel to the shore is an appalling experience – there it is so close and yet it gets no nearer. Why not, what is wrong that we don't immediately head in?

Unfortunately this hanging over the rail led to him falling in on a number of occasions.

This was even more terrifying, luckily the large splash usually attracted our attention, then a little golden head would appear, eyes rolling in dismay, and he would do his best to climb vertically out of the water and back on board.

All these things we learnt about him gradually, but when he was a little over six months old we had to abandon him in kennels for two months whilst we were in England.

Since none of us had ever been separated from each other for more than a few hours at a time before, this was a traumatic experience for us all. We consoled ourselves that at least Fen and Rommel got on well together and would be company or each other.

I had used the same kennels in Harare for a number of years and knew they were reliable, nonetheless I took precautions. At least seven close friends and relatives were made to solemnly swear that they would phone the kennels at least once a week and confirm that all was well.

I reasoned that, reliable they might be, but that in a matter of such paramount importance it would be well to keep reminding them that our eyes were on them.

As far as I know most did phone, and in retrospect my sympathies go to the poor kennel owners who must have been driven berserk. I offer them my apologies now, a little belatedly.

From the dogs side there was no difficulty leaving them that first time. Fenella as always was fascinated by this strange place full of other dogs and smells. Rommel having observed that all the other dogs were securely separated from him by strong mesh felt safe in hurling imprecations at them as he walked past.

We installed them in their run, left numerous blankets, sleeping bags, pillows (and pieces of our worn clothing) and other essentials and departed keeping brave faces. These lasted until we were in the car when we drove off in a mist of tears.

Since those days they have had to go to kennels on a number of occasions, usually for short periods but once for nearly three months. I don't think Rommel minds too much, he goes in quite happily and we leave him growling ferociously at the next door neighbours.

Fenella has no such feelings. She will come with me and examine everything with interest, but as soon as we reach the end of the run and I have to say "Stay", she becomes a picture of abject misery. Down goes her tail between her legs, she sinks quivering onto the floor and looks up at me piteously.

"You can't really be going to do this to me again" she says. I have to, but it breaks my heart every time. Apart from the separation she has my total sympathy, I loathed every day of my long boarding school years as well.

As a rough rule of thumb in the animal world the bigger you are the longer you live. Dogs for some mysterious reason reverse this process. The smaller the dog is the longer its life expectancy. Twelve years old in a big dog is a great age but I know of dachsies still going (if not strong) at eighteen.

Fenella and Rommel are now twelve and eleven and look and behave like dogs half their age. Possibly in recognition of this fact their maker deigned to fit long memories into those little pea sized brains – but at the time we abandoned them in kennels we didn't know his.

Jean always said that of course they wouldn't forget us, but I had my doubts. It would have been too awful to come back and find we were strangers.

My experience with dogs in the past gave mixed results.

I did know that my mother's dachsie, Vicky, had had a remarkable memory. My parents were still in Tanganyika at the time and I had not been home for five years. I drove up from Rhodesia (as it was then), arriving at about two in the afternoon. Vicky was about ten at the time, rebuffed my advances on arrival and would have nothing to do with me. It hardly surprised me after such a long period, especially since she had never been my dog anyway.

Al that afternoon she lay on a chair and gazed at me without, by even a twitch of her tail indicating she heard the odd remark I addressed to her. Then at about five in the evening without any warning, she jumped down, ran over and leapt on my lap and said " Hello". It was indisputable that she had been pondering the matter for some three hours and had finally placed me. It was a remarkable feat of memory.

Zeus, my Alsatian I had no doubt would have recognised me instantaneously even if we had been parted for decades – but then I once owned a red setter!

This was the only puppy I ever got suckered into taking purely on the strength of his looks, or rather his parent's looks. When Thor grew up he was equally magnificent, a dark wine red with slightly wavy brindles showing up in sunlight.

He is also beyond any doubt the stupidest dog I have ever owned. He could accommodate half a thought at a time, to get it into his head took days and once there nothing would ever dislodge it. Learning was virtually beyond him.

When I got him I was living in a Police camp in Rhodesia and already had Zeus. One night these two, accompanied by the Sergeant Major's two hunting dogs descended on the police lines and slaughtered some thirty chickens which were kept there.

This was not only a serious matter in itself but one which required that I should never again be faced with such a bill for compensation – especially on a monthly salary of thirty pounds!

I borrowed one of the few fortunate surviving chickens, tied it to a post on the veranda and called Zeus. He came bounding round the corner, saw the chicken, remembered those deliciously exciting night hours, took one stalking step towards it, then paused for a fraction of a second and looked around him.

There were for or five of us standing there and it only took a further half second for him to work it out for himself – all was not well. The step turned into a smart about turn and an unavailing effort to escape retribution. Yet he had never killed a chicken before or even been disciplined for chasing one. He never did again.

Having disposed of him we called Thor (you may notice that I had a penchant for assorted god names in those days of my youth). He arrived, saw the chicken and ignoring all else stalked it until punishment arrived as he was about to take a mouthful. I had to repeat the experience for five days in a row before he learnt.

I used to take the two out at night onto a disused airstrip to hunt hares. An African hare can do around thirty miles an hour and can stop on a dime. The first time Zeus chased one he was going flat out when the hare stopped. He was about twenty yards on before he realised there was no longer a hare in front of him. Bemused he looked around and saw the hare far off heading in the opposite direction.

From then on he concentrated on staying just behind them until they stopped and then as he went over them one bite despatched them

Thor was all legs – he could do around forty-five miles an hour but it took a little time to get worked up to full speed. He never learnt and never killed one. He would work up to full speed, the hare would stop dead, Thor would continue for twenty yards before he realised it was no longer in front and he attempted to stop and turn.

The ensuing action resembled nothing so much as one of those cartoon drawings which depict a cloud of dust with the odd leg or arm sticking out of it. It was usually dusty - and that was all you saw. Eventually when he had managed to stop and stand up again he would take off again in the new direction with exactly the same result.

At the risk of alienating red setter lovers I have to say that every one I have come across since has been much the same.

When he was three (Thor) we went to England for two months. By this time I really felt that I could do without him, a local farmer wanted him as a guard dog and would give him an excellent home so I gave him away.

About a week after our return I visited the farmer on a patrol to be met by Thor (now with a good Afrikaans name) who came up barking furiously and prepared to attack me. When he was a few yards away something about my voice did penetrate the impenetrable mists and he came to a dubious halt. But he didn't really remember me at all.

Would Fen and Rommel?

I need not have worried. My memories of my holiday are vague but the high point of it all was collecting the dogs. It took us just long enough to get off the plane, collect the car and drive straight to the kennels.

Out they came, Fenella leapt at me, then Jean, then went into a frenzy of displacement activity. Rommel hesitated for a fraction of a second then did the same. Considering that he had been in the kennels for a quarter of his whole life, he could be forgiven a second's hesitation.

Nor have we ever worried since. Rommel is not given to rapturous welcomes with anyone except Jean or me, but Fenella gives them to all close family. Alex had been away on and off for years, boarding school, nursing and finally two years globe trotting. The second Fen set eyes on her at the airport she was all over her.

It was also a relief that I hadn't been sent to Coventry, she had first done this about six months before we left.

I had had to leave her behind for a day and had looked forward to my welcome on my return – no such thing awaited me. Rommel was pleased to see me – but Fenella ….!

She started towards me and after a few steps stopped dead. "So you've come back at last" she might almost have spoken "you leave me behind abandoned with that woman and that other dog and now I suppose I'm expected to give you a big welcome. Well if you think you can get away with that sort of behaviour, you can think again."

She turned round and walked stiff legged back to the house without a backward glace. What's more for twelve hours no quantity of blandishments had the slightest effect. Not only would she not come to me, but she wouldn't even listen to me.

If she was facing me and I spoke to her she actually turned her head away, if I continued she would turn around and walk off. She had done it a couple of times subsequently although for briefer periods. The thought of what she would consider a suitable term of excommunication in punishment for a two month abandonment terrified me.

Fortunately this period was simply too long, and in fact she never did it again.

We returned to Kariba and ran into a new problem with the dogs – baboons. The baboons of Africa flourish, clever, quick to exploit any easy food source, and with possibly the best troop organisation of any animal, they are a pest.

The members of the two troops living around the town were also without doubt the fattest and sleekest in Africa. They had adapted to a semi-urban life style and improved meals with such items as loaves of bread, with gusto.

A big dog baboon is a fearsome animal, sitting around four feet high with huge canine teeth, strong jaws and powerful hands and feet. In Kariba they were only mildly apprehensive of men and totally unafraid of women or children.

Jean learnt this soon after our arrival there. She had some papaya trees growing in the garden and the baboons infuriated her by breaking off the tender tops. She looked out one day to see a big dog baboon at the last surviving tree. Seizing a tennis racquet she tore out waving it and shouting imprecations. The baboon looked up calmly, broke off the tree (it was only about five feet high) and shook it back at Jean who retired in disorder back into the house.

The next time they were in the garden she was so incensed that she took out our 12 bore shotgun. The troop ignored the pointed weapon and the ineffectual bang-bang sounds she was making. Her temper snapped and pointing the gun into the air she let off a round. She was horrified when a baboon dropped from a nearby tree and lay lifeless on the ground. She didn't pause to consider how strange it was, in view of the fact that she hadn't been pointing the gun at anything except the sky!

She started towards it (I can only imagine to render first aid) but when she was a few yards away it leapt unscathed to its feet and headed after the rest of the troop who had meanwhile made their escape.

It was a system that this particular troop had devised. If a shot was fired near them at least one, and sometimes two or three would drop down and feign death. Whilst occasionally the hunters must have been perplexed at their success, particularly when they killed a baboon in a different direction from the one which they were aiming at, invariably they stopped shooting and went to investigate. By the time they discovered their error the troop was gone.

A demonstration of their powers of observation came from the Game Guards. These were the only people who they feared as occasionally they would have to try and shoot a few to keep numbers down. They wore a green uniform with epaulettes on their shoulders. One sight of one of these in uniform and the troop would disappear. An old hunter told them to take off their epaulettes (they were obliged to wear the uniform), they did so and for a short period had great success – the baboons no longer fled on sight, the one small change to the uniform rendered it unidentifiable to them.

The greatest problem with them was theft. They once made use of a broken pane in the club kitchen to lift the latch, open the window and gain access. The mess inside was indescribable. The local bakery waged a non stop war with them, leave a truck, bakery door or window open and unattended for a minute and they were in.

When this happened any passers-by were treated to an astounding sight. Strings of baboons with pleased smiles running off two legged, whilst each carried a loaf or two of bread tucked under each armpit. Bread was the baboons' idea of manna from heaven, not infrequently they would actually rob smaller children returning home alone with a loaf of bread.

When I was in my teens living in an Africa which no longer exists, my idea of paradise was a place I could wander through with a gun killing everything that moved. I not only grew out of it, but nowadays have a positive aversion to killing anything, but with the baboons we had no choice.

It wasn't just that if Jean was alone in the kitchen, they would actually come into the house, it was the dogs. Normally they will run from dogs, but even one on one any mature baboon is more than a match for the largest dog and there are plenty of instances where a dog has got too close to the heartland of the troop and been literally torn to pieces. When you consider that there are plenty of recorded occasions of baboons attacking leopards which threatened the troop, it is not surprising that dogs don't inspire much fear. Even a three month old baboon could have killed Rommel or Fenella in seconds.

As both dogs would try and attack them, one had to keep them out of the garden.

Excellent though the troops' communication system is, their memory is unfortunately limited.

Finally when we were being overrun I would have to shoot one, I ensured that I always did this within our fenced garden. The troop had the message within hours. For six months they would pass by but no baboon would come over the fence. Then slowly the teenagers became braver and began to venture back. At this stage it was only necessary to grab a broom or straight stick and point it at them to effect their immediate departure.

Over the next few months they would become more daring, broomstick and cries of "Bang Bang" would be ignored and you had to get the shotgun out and work the bolt. This was still effective.

At last even this no longer caught their attention and I had to shoot one again. The whole cycle took close to eighteen months.

Incidentally for those purists who are saying 'Shotgun? Bolt' I owned a Savage bolt action 12 bore shotgun, the only shotgun with that action I have ever come across.

Now the dogs were back and Rommel a bit bigger, they would both go berserk when the baboons were nearby. Outside the garden I made sure that they didn't chase them too far, but inside there wasn't much that I could do. The baboons stayed outside the fence and the dogs tore along inside in a frenzy of fury.

It evolved into a game although it was some time before the dogs viewed it in that light.

I went out one day to find three young baboons sitting on the path running along outside the fence. They were squatting on their back legs holding their front ones up above their heads rather in the attitude of a man surrendering to the enemy. At the same time they hopped up and down making faces and noises through the wire to tease the dogs.

The dogs were not surprisingly in a state of apoplexy. Eventually though, they entered into the spirit of it as well and the performance continued all the years we were in that house. The younger baboons learnt it from their elders, but the funny thing was the adult baboons.

The juveniles began it but over the course of time they grew into full sized adults, but they still played their youthful pranks.

It wasn't long before we found fully grown baboons sitting on the path and bobbing up and down with their hands in the air. When they saw you it was impossible not to decry a certain sheepishness in their demeanour as they fled. They looked ridiculous, like a man caught unaware playing childish games.

It worried Jean enormously, but in fact the whole performance had become so stylised on both sides that I always felt the participants knew the rules and would abide by them. Thankfully they did.

We settled back in. Rommel continued to try and catch other dogs to savage them, both chased baboons and any cats they saw, except Cat. Cat hated Rommel as much as Fenella and accorded him the same cavalier treatment.

When at last she disappeared, we never found any trace of her. I think a bigger predator caught her, but Jean has always believed that the dogs finally cornered her outside the house and killed her. If they did she certainly reaped her own whirlwind.

Later in the year Fenella came on heat for the first time.

Our sleeping arrangements were now settled. Jean and I slept back to back in the centre of the bed, Rommel slept on Jean's side and Fenella curled up in my tummy or stretched out with her head on my shoulder.

She was also very good about respecting my right to sleep. Fenella is not a slug-a-bed, she likes to be up about and doing interesting things, so she usually woke well before I did, but she won't disturb me, she lies and watches me carefully, as long as I keep my eyelids firmly closed she will stay still and quiet – however – let me blink even one eyelid momentarily and we are up.

"Thank God you're awake at last" she says "now we can get up and go and do something interesting".

I am not allowed to sink back into slumber. It took me a little while to catch on to this system, then if I wanted to lie in a while I made sure my eyes remained firmly shut until I was ready to face the day!

Fenella doesn't always like to be cuddled, but she does like to have some physical contact with me when she sleeps, usually this is her backside.

She has always been nervous about her hindquarters and for many years even Jean wasn't allowed to touch her back legs without being snapped at.

There has never been anything wrong with them that I know of and I came to the conclusion that it was purely because they were a long way (by dachsie standards) from her head, and she feared that something would happen to them before she had time to notice.

I confess that this theory arose out of a story told me years before by my parents about the larger dinosaurs. This was that if you had bitten a dinosaur's tail it would have taken about five minutes for the message to reach their brain because of the distance involved. I have never checked up on this but with the benefit of increased years and knowledge I am rather reluctantly forced to conclude that I was lied to as a child. Luckily I don't think that it has had too severe effect on my neuroses, and at least the story provided me with a possible solution to Fenella's problem.

It was naturally impossible to explain to Fenella that when she was on heat she would have to sleep elsewhere than in my bed, and in practice the few minute blood spots that resulted were hardly a problem.

Fenella is talkative, to have consigned her to another room at night would have meant no sleep for us or anyone living nearby.

Rommel is the strong silent type – so he got locked out. Whilst he is not vocal Rommel is an action dog. For nearly three weeks he spent eight hours a night trying to dig his way through the bottom of the bedroom door. These efforts were accompanied by suitable grunts and groans of determination.

He didn't succeed but neither did we get much sleep. Next time she came on heat we agreed we would let them mate. At least this would mean that we wouldn't have to keep them apart, they would be welcome to indulge in orgies of sex all day and night long and we would get some peace.

Little did we understand our dogs? We thought that the hideous experience of keeping them apart had been bad – it was nothing compared to the exhaustion caused to us by days of consummation.

We prepared ourselves. All the vets we knew were consulted. As the time approached for Fen to come on heat we began stuffing her in advance with vitamin and calcium tablets, her diet began to revolve around raw liver and other similar delicacies packed with iron.

At last The Day came. Once she was well on heat Rommel proved to require no sexual counselling and performed admirably. Fenella whilst only moderately enamoured of the process bore with it all patiently.

We congratulated ourselves that apart from the danger of tripping over copulating dachshunds, all would be well and peaceful. Unfortunately we had not taken into account Fenella's deeply ingrained sense of right and wrong.

We retired to bed on the first night with everyone in their accustomed places and fell into a blameless slumber.

Shortly afterwards I was half woken by Rommel walking across my feet from his side of the bed. A few seconds later my stomach erupted under the blanket with series of ferocious snarls and growls... Rommel retired discomforted and I tried to get my heartbeat back to close to normal.

Fenella has a very proper sense of time and place, as should any lady. Sex may be patiently born with or even enjoyed during the day, this she considered culturally correct. The night was a different matter, who had ever heard of sex in the dark? The night was there for rest and sleep, she was comfortable and relaxed in her usual position and had no intention of letting other dogs, even Rommel disturb her.

It was worse than having Rommel locked out. He may not be the most intelligent of dogs, but love can spur the imagination. Having been repulsed from the bottom of the bed he decided that the answer would be to approach from a different direction.

No sooner had I drifted off again when I was woken by him creeping stealthily across my middle, this in itself was quite painful as he is no lightweight and his weight is concentrated in his paws rather like a woman in high heels.

I was too late to stop Fenella rejecting him again with another ferocious display.

We sorted everyone out and tried to settle down again.

Rommel had now tried two approaches and failed. Nothing dismayed he tried again. This time I was woken by a paw in my eye as he crept surreptitiously across the pillows. As the rear paw entered my mouth (never sleep with your mouth open is the moral) I was quick enough to catch him before Fenella tried to kill him again.

Still unbeaten, having tried every angle of approach across the bed he now got off it and on tiptoe crept round via the floor to my side. Having reached a point opposite Fenella he ran into a problem.

Rommel is not a good leaper. Fen's back is supple and supplies the power when she is running or jumping upwards. Rommel's strength is in his massive shoulders and chest. Jumping up onto things such as chairs or beds requires a push from the back end, Rommel has little faith in the strength of his hindquarters and thus he needs to prepare himself psychologically.

Faced with a jump which he is dubious about, he stands in front of whatever it is and makes little bounces on his front paws until he has summoned the courage to attempt the leap. This makes a little pat, pat sound as his front paws hit the ground after each bounce.

He is very sensitive about this failing, no doubt some of it being our fault. Occasionally after the necessary number of bounces he has tried and failed, viewed from any point of view except Rommel's it is the funniest sight and it was almost impossible not to burst into mirth.

This both embarrassed and upset him. If you laughed he knew you had noticed and would walk firmly away pretending that he never really intended to get on that thing at all. "I never actually meant it" he said "I just thought I'd have a small bounce and a quick look."

If you didn't laugh it was essential to look firmly in another direction, because as soon as he had recovered his feet, he would look round anxiously to see if anyone had noticed. Only if he was sure that you hadn't would he try again.

The bed was just within his reach but needed a lot of mental preparation, the 'pat pat' woke me and I caught him in time again. We got even less sleep.

All hopes of a peaceful night were dachsied. Rommel was once more locked out of the bedroom. On the previous occasions he had wanted to get in instinctively – now he *knew* why and the pleasures that hopefully awaited him. His determination was redoubled as were his grunts of effort as he tried to demolish the door.

Had there been a kennels within three hundred miles I would have cheerful consigned both to it by this time, there wasn't, so we gritted our teeth and resigned ourselves. Never again, I swore, was I going to go through this performance.

Eventually all passed, nights became peaceful again disturbed only by Fenella's snores and snuffles. She does this even worse than Jean but then she has a longer Roman nose! It would probably drive anyone else mad but I am so used to it that I never notice.

She also had a waist that I could encircle with the fingers of one hand. We watched it with greater attention than any new Queen ever received whilst the kingdom awaited an heir.

In the meantime we continued to stuff her with pills and fancy tonics.

Chapter Three

"There is sorrow enough in the natural way
For men and women to fill our day
And when we are certain of sorrow in store,
Why do we always arrange for more?
Brothers and sisters, I bid you beware
Of giving your heart to a dog to tear".

R. Kipling

It wasn't long before there was a noticeable thickening and her teats started to fill out. The daily panic got worse and the number of pills and supplementary feeds got greater.

Seldom if ever, has a mother with her first child been so nervously coddled and examined. If I could have found a pre-natal clinic for dachshunds I would have sent her there.

The real problem was where we should put her with her puppies, this had to be in our bedroom as if she was anywhere else I wouldn't be able to trust her not to abandon the puppies for the night and come to bed with me. Three feet from the side of my bed was a built in cupboard with a convenient compartment in the bottom. This was filled with the usual sleeping bags, pillows and other comforts essential to a young mother.

Fenella investigated, found it interesting but saw no reason to sleep in it or stay there when all her normal beds and chairs were available.

My next concern was where she would have them. As she insisted on accompanying me everywhere this could be anywhere from the seat of the car to a picnic spot in the bush. In fact I was certain she would give birth sometime around midnight.

I had grounds for this. Every bitch I have ever owned always gave birth between midnight and 2 am. Other people may own well trained bitches that have puppies at convenient times of the day – not I!

Molly my Alsatian bitch, slept under the head of the bed. This was convenient as when she gave birth in the middle of the night you simply pulled the bed out a couple of feet and you could look over or reach down to ensure all was well with only a minimum of effort.

I knew the exact place Fenella would consider ideal – my tummy. Unless I woke up smartly I could see myself surfacing in a welter of puppies. I didn't fancy it. As the time got closer I became an increasingly light and nervous sleeper, the slightest twitch from Fen brought me awake instantaneously to check on her.

Sure enough at midnight one night I was woken by Fenella turning round and round obviously in some discomfort. A brief examination revealed that it seemed likely that the great event was about to take place.

I transferred her gently to the bottom of the cupboard and sat with her until the first puppy was born (naturally I never dreamed of doing this with my wife!). It was a long labour and we didn't get much sleep that night, the fourth and last puppy was born at eight o'clock in the morning.

I have to say that she managed it all with exemplary calm, all four were healthy with the necessary appendages, two were black and tan and two were tan. They were unbelievably tiny and could have been any breed. Each was some two inches long with minute legs, unformed heads and round blobs of ears that stood up like an Alsatians.

Jean claimed Fen wasn't a good mother, this was slander (or libel whichever is which!). She may not have very strong maternal instincts but she did everything necessary to look after the pups. For the first three days she wouldn't let anyone else, even Jean handle the puppies. I was permitted but she watched nervously.

Damnit and Rommel (both interested) weren't allowed into the passage to the bedroom, much less the bedroom. This caused some dissension as Rommel, in particular, was keenly interested in what was going on and kept trying to sneak down for a quick look.

After a week she relaxed a little, Rommel still wasn't allowed into the room but he could get as far as the door. At night she began hopping back into bed with me but the minute a puppy cried she was straight back to them.

The puppies were extraordinary, in the first week they doubled in length and within two weeks their noses began to grow, their ears flopped and they were recognisable dachsies. At about this time I admit that Fenella began to show a noticeable diminution in maternal responsibilities.

"Feed them – yes" you could hear her saying "but for how long am I expected to remain tied to these things?"

They became mobile and we started taking them into the lounge, like all new things they were entrancing. Fen was nervous at first but soon got used to other people and dogs round them.

It was at this stage that we discovered we had the wrong mother. Rommel adored them. It wasn't simply that he was fascinated by them, but he loved them and wanted to be with them the whole time. It took him some time and a lot of patience and many cautious approaches before Fenella actually let him sniff and touch one. Once he had, she decided that he could be trusted and let him carry on.

By now she felt her duty had been done and it was time she resumed a normal life accompanying me again. She made sure that they were fed and in safe surroundings and considered that to be compatible with her responsibilities. Rommel took over.

The second Fen left them he joined them, nor would he leave them alone. He was amazingly careful and gentle. If they were crawling all over him and he wanted to get up, he did so an inch at a time so that no-one fell off.

All this showed splendid restraint because the puppies had teeth like scalpels. Our hands were scratched to ribbons, it wasn't that they bit you, but if a tooth was drawn gently across the skin it sliced it open. How Fen could bear to feed them I don't know.

By now Rommel spent more time with them than Fenella, so the puppies viewed him as a second mother. This led to a painful and embarrassing experience.

I came into the lounge one evening to find three puppies playing happily with each other and Rommel stalking very slowly around the walls, moving stiff legged and apparently in great pain. Of the fourth puppy there was no sign.

I didn't know what was wrong with Rommel but the whereabouts of the other puppy seemed more important. I looked for it anxiously, then just as I was becoming seriously worried, I saw it.

It had become hungry and in Fenella's absence sought an alternative source of milk supply. Rommel presumably had one, nor had it sought in vain. With its teeth firmly locked it was hanging on to his penis. It must have been agony for Rommel, his eyes were nearly closed and he wore an expression compounded of suffering and despair.

I detached it as gently as possible and the look of relief on his face was almost comic. He took care that it never happened again.

I had intended to let Fen have two litters, but despite the supplementary diet she produced so much milk that her body couldn't keep up and on two or three occasions she had minor convulsions brought on by a calcium deficiency. This also cost a fortune in panic phone calls to the vet. I resolved to have her spayed as soon as she was well enough. I have a feeling that she was greatly relieved.

We now came to the puppy disposal and finding good homes, Jean was weakening but I remained adamant.

Many years before a great dog lover I knew told me never to give a puppy or dog away, always make a charge, even if it was nominal. Her reasoning made sense. It was simply that people never value anything they get free. Puppies are adorable and they wanted one at the time. Later when it grew up, chewed things and generally became a nuisance they lost interest, ceased to care for it and probably gave it away to anyone who would have it

If they paid for it, it became an object with a value attached. Objects of value are better cared for and looked after.

My mother at one time bred West Highland whites. These were highly pedigreed and sold for large sums – provided you were lucky enough to get one. As far as I could ascertain the procedure went something like this:-

The puppies were advertised and you phoned up and gave your address. Any hope you had of merely finding out if one was available and collecting it, disappeared at this stage. You then received a four page questionnaire covering such details as dogs owned, size of garden, how many rooms in the house, what plants you grew, children and ages, any diseases any of you might have had which were communicable to canines, your income, job and other pertinent questions about your private life. A minimum of four referees with impeccable dog credentials were also obligatory.

You filled this in and returned it. Once all applications had been minutely scrutinised and, if you were fortunate enough to make the shortlist, you received a phone call summoning you to an interview. My mother grilled you for an hour or so, and if she considered you as potential parent, you might actually be allowed to view the puppies, though not of course, to buy or choose one! Then you were sent home to await results.

Finally the lucky few received a message giving you a date and time for collection and reminding you to bring a large cheque with you.

Having survived all this and collected your puppy you might have been pardoned for believing that it was now yours.

Not at all.

My mother's senses were far in excess of five. On one occasion waking in the early hours of the morning one of them told her clearly that she had made a mistake with one puppy. My father was woken; money collected and after a two hundred mile drive the puppy recovered from its new home and the unfortunate owners.

Those who think that they might have refused to hand it back have never encountered my mother. She was not a woman to be trifled with.

We didn't go quite to these extremes but we were as careful as we could be and as all the potential owners were known to us personally we hoped we had got it right. Each puppy went with a two page owners' manual on its care and maintenance.

We did have to recover one when the owner suddenly left the country and couldn't take it, but that was all. This was in fact the prettiest puppy and the spitting image of Fenella, getting Jean to part with her a second time was a major battle.

I arranged to have Fen spayed the next time the vet was up in Kariba. Not knowing what was in store for her Fen was unconcerned, we on the other hand were. She had never had an anaesthetic before and you never know how they will react. Molly, my Alsatian bitch, had died under one. She was apparently as fit as a fiddle but I was also having her spayed and it turned out she had a minor heart defect and the anaesthetic was too much for it.

Nowadays both dogs view vets' surgeries with the same feelings as children (and most adults) view dentists. Experience has taught that the things that are likely to happen to you there are invariably unpleasant.

Fenella is marvellous with me if anything is wrong and will let me look and touch without complaining – but vets are another mater. However this was the first occasion apart from a couple of jabs, so she wasn't too apprehensive. I took her in and stayed with her until she passed out.

Three hours later I collected her – still out cold. Vets tend to like to keep animals at their surgeries until they are sure they are recovered. This is understandable and in some cases possibly necessary, but I prefer to take mine home as soon as possible.

Shock is a big factor with any operation and with animals perhaps even greater than with people, who at least know what it was all about when they come round. The combination of shock and awaking sore and disorientated in a strange place, particularly one which has unpleasant connotations can put a major brake on their progress to recovery and sometimes even kill.

We had learnt this the hard way. We had had a small fox terrier, a rescued stray, who after a number of years got a growth the size of a tennis ball on his side. It didn't appear to hurt him but the size was becoming a nuisance and it was still growing. After consultations with the vet we decided to have it removed. We had no idea how old he was, and he certainly wasn't a young dog, on the other hand he was fit and in good condition.

We had grossly underestimated the trauma caused by an operation. He recovered from it but the vet said they want to keep him for observation in their kennels so they could monitor his recovery and we agreed.

He never recovered properly and lingered on there and died five days later. I was convinced that had we taken him home he would have, if not actually recovered, at least stood a far better chance of doing so in an environment that he knew and felt safe in. I never forgave myself for not doing so and overriding the vet, and vowed never to repeat the mistake.

I know no more pathetic sight than an unconscious dog. Perhaps it is because they are more lively than people when conscious that the contrast seems greater. She flopped limp in my arms with her tongue dangling out of one side of her mouth.

I was assured that she would come round shortly but would remain heavily doped and unsteady for a considerable length of time. As there seemed to be no danger of her coming round and jumping off, we put her on the bed in the air-conditioned bedroom (Kariba temperatures especially in summer were often in the 40sC) and took turns sitting with her. She came round briefly, recognised us, wagged her tail and drifted off again.

All seemed well and I had to go out in the car. This was parked some thirty yards from the house. I went over to it got in and started the engine, then there was a petrified cry from Jean, I looked round in time to see Fenella emerge from the house at a run (albeit a little wobbly) and head for the car.

I picked her up sure that she must have torn her stitches or damaged herself, but all seemed well and her tail wagged furiously. Doped or not she had recognised the sound of our car engine. I was going SOMEWHERE WITHOUT HER! This was unthinkable and brought her round immediately. She settled on the car seat happily, obviously convinced that all was now well with the world again.

"Thought you'd leave me" she said "well think again, here I am and I'm coming as usual."

She did.

By that evening she was wandering around, a little stiffly but not in any apparent great discomfort. The vet very kindly came round to the house in the evening before he left town, to check she was alright. We stood on the veranda.

"Don't worry," he said "if she stays doped for some time and doesn't want to move much because she's sore. She'll soon recover."

Without a sound I pointed to his feet. Fenella was standing by him sniffing his trousers and looking perfectly fit. I don't know which he was most – gratified or surprised.

She also showed remarkable good sense later when it came to the time to remove her stitches.

I had been given careful instructions about these, but I fear that I am not a natural doctor. When I was young and single and owned Zeus, my Alsatian, the places I lived in were far beyond the call of a vet. At that age I was also sure that I knew the answer to everything anyway.

If Zeus had a problem of any kind I would visit the nearest little rural clinic and borrow a large syringe and a dose of penicillin. On the face of it giving an injection would seem a simple operation. Stick the needle in, depress the plunger, pull the needle out and Bob's your uncle.

Alex tells me that when she was a student nurse they practised first on oranges. Even then when the dread day came and one of their numbers was confronted with a bared live backside and a hypodermic, her nerve broke and she burst into wails of "No no I can't do it."

What the unfortunate patient thought she didn't say, but the story left me with a firm resolve to never let myself be admitted to a teaching hospital.

At the time though, Alex wasn't even thought of, and no-one had told me about oranges. I practised on Zeus, especially to begin with this was a painful experience – for Zeus. Giving an injection through thick fur is even harder than into a nice smooth backside. One result of this was that Zeus conceived an aversion to syringes. If he had to have an injection you needed to make sure that he was fully secured before anyone touched a syringe. Let him get one glimpse of this dread instrument and he would be gone, not only gone but he would make sure he stayed hidden for at least four hours or so, until he thought that the danger had passed.

Taking stitches out sounds equally straight forward, again it is not. They have to be cut in the right places and pulled from the correct ends, you have to be sufficiently firm without being rough. Be too gentle and all you cause is discomfort without removing the stitch.

I viewed the removal of Fenella's with trepidation, not so much because I didn't think I was capable, as in case I was clumsy and hurt her unnecessarily.

The morning dawned – I had a look and said to Jean that I would do them after lunch as I was busy that morning. After lunch we gathered together scissors tweezers, cotton wool, and rolls of bandages (in case…), rolled up our sleeves and called Fenella.

Not one single piece of stitch remained, she had taken them all out that morning herself and left me nothing to do.

Perhaps she had just decided that now was the right time, but I prefer to think that a little ESP took place and that she decided in the circumstances that it would be safer to do it herself!

How wise she was, was demonstrated a few years later when I had to take some stitches out of Rommel who had had a minor operation. I removed them, I thought adequately, then for six months little pieces of stitch which I had left in would appear and have to be hauled out.

The puppy episode was now closed, although Fenella never quite recovered her eighteen inch waist, and we did keep an eye on the puppies out of interest.

Two went to one woman and unfortunately got stolen, we could only hope that the people who wanted them badly enough to steal them would also look after them, the one passed out of our area and the last, a black and tan dog went to an old friend of ours who had recently lost his dog.

He was a bachelor and was besotted with his new puppy, this was just as well as the puppy rather unfortunately demonstrated that not everything in Rommel's ancestry had been perfect. He was a sort of cross between his parents, singly the pieces looked alright, but put together you always got the impression that something was not quite legitimate even if you couldn't put your finger on it.

He also inherited Fenella's hunting instincts together with his father's thought processes – or lack of. This combination led him into some painful situations.

Kariba like Rome is built on seven hills – but these are more precipitous ones – with the result that many of the houses on the heights are built on platforms cut out of the side of the hill. Go out the back door and you find yourself on a six foot wide strip with a retaining wall rising as far as the eaves. John, his owner, lived in one of these, and there was about a foot wide gap between the bottom of the roof and the top of the retaining wall.

At one end of the house there was a tree whose smaller branches reached the roof, from which there was an eight foot drop into a flower bed.

Kariba abounded in squirrels, an animal which his latest acquisition was confident he could deal with if only he could get to close quarters with one.

Down the hill came the squirrels, closely pursued by the dog, hopped onto the roof, followed by the dog, ran along the roof to the end and leapt into the tree – followed by the dog.

It is sad to record that dachshund paws are not suitable or tree work. Tarzan may have adapted but not the dachsie, with the consequence that he then fell eight feet into the flower bed – and he did it more than once, luckily he never hurt himself.

The only moral of this story that I can think of is that compromises have their problems.

Fenella is too intelligent, no matter what the excitement; she retains a sense of self preservation and would have stopped at the roof edge. Rommel on the other hand is too slow physically to have kept up with the squirrels in the first place and would have lost track of them long before they reached the roof.

Chapter Four

'Master – again Thy Servant! This that was once Thy Shoe,
He has found and taken and carried aside, as a fitting matter to chew.
Now there is neither blacking nor tongue, and the Housemaid has us in tow.
Master remember Thy Servant is young, and tell her to let him go.'

R. Kipling

Like all parents we used to play games with the children, and we did with the dachsies too. These were of the type where an ecstatic feeling of terror is produced followed by expected relief when all ends well.

With Fenella it was 'The Wild Woods'. This was not complicated. You approached her with a fierce face and spoke in a deep growly voice "I'M COMING TO TAKE YOU TO THE WILD WOODS' you said.

She would be absolutely petrified with pleasurable fear and would roll on her back, head stretched out and tail wagging furiously. Then you went close and said in her ear 'To pick mushrooms' in a high falsetto.

This was followed immediately by a roar of '**NO TO EAT YOU', and you grabbed her at the same time.** The excitement was marvellous and she would leap up and tear around the room a few times and when the displacement activity had worked off enough energy, come back and lie down hopefully on her back for it all to be repeated.

Rommel was not a satisfactory participant. I fancy he is too much of a pessimist at heart and was never certain that he was actually going to survive it all. However, he is so phlegmatic that it is difficult to tell. When all was finished his tail would wag a couple of times, he would roll his eyes nervously and look vaguely surprised that he was still in one piece. As a playmate he has his drawbacks.

We have all matured and no longer play it as such, but Fenella developed her own game which she still likes to play. Occasionally when the excitement got too much she would half snap at your nose and this led to a variation, you growled at her 'Did you try and bite my nose' falsetto 'Do you know what happens to dogs who bite people's noses' and finally 'They get their noses bitten'.

It was the same game with one variation and that was that she could initiate it when she wanted to play, She does this by pointing her nose in the air and making tiny snapping motions in the vague direction of your face. It is still her favourite game and I am often required to play.

Rommel watches it all with the disdain of an adult for a child.

A few years later we moved to Malawi and Fenella learnt a new game. For the first time she was unable to come to work with me as there was a large car park and I was afraid she would get run over. At first she was dismayed when I left, and would sit and howl at the gate, then she learnt patience and would wait to greet me with wild exuberance when she saw me coming. Finally she became blasé and merely remained in her chair in the lounge.

When I get home naturally I said 'Hello' to Fenella first, then Rommel and finally to Jean.

Fenella remained in her chair like royalty, tail wagging and waited for me to come over and greet her. This made me so mad that I decided to teach her a lesson. The next time I came home I said hellos to Rommel, kissed Jean, made a fuss of both and ignored Fen. Then without looking at her I said "Where's Fen"

By this time she was wriggling on the chair, thoroughly perturbed, she is at the best of times excessively jealous, and here I was ignoring her. I went through the house calling her in a louder and louder and more and more desperate voice.

For a short while she remained in her chair convinced that I *really* knew where she was, then doubt set in and the situation became unbearable, she leapt down and followed me from room to room, tail almost coming off with the force of its wagging. At last I noticed her and made a big fuss. She went almost berserk.

"You stupid man, couldn't you see I was here all the time" she said.

It became a standard game and she understood it. She is a vocal dog, if she wants or needs something she is not backward in telling you. Until I 'found' her she would never utter a sound, nor would she touch me, it was part of the game.

All this was naturally far below Rommel's level of maturity. Even Fenella finds him an inadequate playmate. Once in a while she gets kittenish and bounces round him in invitation. Sometimes he will acknowledge her presence and when younger would even participate occasionally. Nowadays if she gets the odd gravity loaded bounce out of him she is doing well.

Poor Rommel, it is funny how often things go wrong for people (like me) who expect them to.

I once read a theory that if you expect something unpleasant to occur, then you subconsciously put yourself in the way of it – and it does.

When we're sailing, Jean always expects a gale – no matter what the forecast. Possibly she has some justification for this as for many years every time I took her out in a new boat one would blow up without warning. Nonetheless I think she manages to conjure them up out of the tiniest fluffiest cloud – by the sheer power of unwishful thinking.

Rommel having little reason to fear anything, is the same; as a consequence things happen to him.

An example of this is 'buzzers'.

A 'buzzer' is a large flying insect which buzzes when it flies. In Africa there are many ranging from hornets, wasps and lethal bees to a large assortment of flies of various sizes. Most buzzy sounding ones sting or bite, some ferociously.

When he was young they didn't perturb him and he used to try and catch them. Then they started stinging him in retaliation, finally word must have got around and they just stung him. It was uncanny, most insects only bite if disturbed, but Rommel could be lying peacefully asleep, one would settle on him and ……ZAP.

He would leap up with howl and need first aid.

To begin with he merely associated stings with the buzzy sound, but over the course of time, as more and more varied insects bite him, he came to associate stings with all large flying insects. The faintest buzzing sound sends him scurrying for cover with his tail between his legs in a state of panic and the same happens if he catches sight of a large flying insect.

It is a sane response because if he stays there, they invariably bite him.

His most terrifying experience occurred many years later on the river

Main in springtime Bavaria. The dragonflies hatched out. A dragonfly may be harmless – but to someone who has never seen one it's a nightmare. Large, coloured and with a massive tail which must evidently harbour an enormous sting.

One flew over the cockpit of the boat, Rommel saw it and nearly broke his neck in his haste to get down the companionway into the cabin and underneath the table. There he remained for nearly an hour, eyes rolling in apprehension as he tried to see if it had followed him. It took a major effort to soothe him and at last persuade him out again.

Fenella, of course, doesn't expect anything to happen to her. She snaps at buzzers, occasionally catches one and yet has only once been bitten by a wasp she caught. This merely redoubled her determination to kill any she saw.

She did at one stage develop a thing about motorbikes, even the sound of one in the distance would drive her mad and if she saw one in motion she tried to catch it. Like dogs who chase cars I found it impossible to break her of the habit.

It nearly broke Fenella.

A young man on a bike, going too fast, entered the car park at the club, Fen went for him, he tried to avoid her but hit her in the stomach. She fled screaming to the house.

We went over her as carefully as possible, she had run back and nothing seemed to be actually broken, although she was very sore. Then within an hour it became apparent that she was very ill and in great pain, and she stiffened, unable to move.

We phoned the vet got prescriptions, collected them and pushed a range of pills into her. The next morning she was no better. On the second day I risked driving her the four hundred odd miles into Harare. She had severe bruising and some internal bleeding, I left with a new selection of more powerful and even more expensive drugs.

There were five vets in that practice and every morning when I phoned I got a different one. Each listened patiently, said "Yes the drugs the previous one had given her were very good, but thought we might do better with these." We got them and paid and she remained the same, apparently hovering between life and death, very sore and unable to move.

On the fifth day Fenella showed no change, but Jean and I were both approaching a state where we needed medical and psychiatric treatment and my bank manger was beginning to phone me about my overdraft.

I phoned and got the fifth vet who again listened carefully whilst I described the variety of drugs she had taken and her condition. He asked about blood in her urine and when the accident had happened. Up until then I think he had assumed that it had occurred within the last couple of days, when told him it was nearly a week before his attitude changed.

"Well" he said "personally I suggest you stop all drugs and leave her to heal herself. If she's still alive after all this time, then she'll probably be fine in a few days."

We took his advice and sure enough within twenty-four hours she was walking around, albeit a little stiffly, but clearly well on her way to recovery.

Since then she has left motorbikes alone.

When the children were small I thought at one time of writing a book entitled 'Life is a NO'. Fortunately for everyone it never progressed beyond the title.

"Daddy please may I go to….." they would say.

"No" we would say firmly, imagining a series of improbable disasters.

"Daddy please may…"

You suddenly found yourself saying 'NO' before you even found out what they wanted.

This was patently ridiculous and as bad for the kids as us, so we made a resolution (and I think stuck to it) to listen to requests and only answer when we had considered them on their merits.

I tried to adopt the same policy when calling the dogs, that is I only called them when I had a specific reason. If I merely wanted to see what they were doing, then I went and had a look.

I have never been a great trainer of dogs although with the big ones it was necessary to make sure that they were reasonably disciplined and obedient. As anyone who has had them will know obedience is not a dachsie trait. Doubtless some of those marvellous people who appear on television could teach them to jump through hoops, but it is beyond me. With a dachshund you're lucky if it comes when you call it and should it have other things on its mind at the time – like hunting –you stand no chance at all.

They are reasonably obedient with me. Jean they refuse to listen to at all. I attribute this to the fact that she was always worrying about them and if they were out of sight would call them back to check on them. At first they came, then when neither food, treats nor anything more interesting than a pat was vouchsafed, they simply said 'To hell with it, we're busy and can't waste time on interruptions.'

Of course it takes time even when they do come, Rommel's idea of obedience is to amble in your direction at a slow waddle with frequent pauses to check on any smells he may have missed on his way out!

Fenella in her favourite lookout spot in the car window

Rommel with his bone

Fenella after a swim with Jean

Rommel as the caring father

Jean and dogs returning from a widdle stop on the Danube in 'Pot'

Fenella's racing dive – the Yacht Club swimming pool, Kariba, Zimbabwe.

The family! – Dogs and us on Rainbow in Kaynarpinar, Gulf of Izmir, Turkey

Chapter Five

> *'Master extol Thy Servant, he has met a most worthy foe!*
> *There has been fighting all over the Shop- and into the Shop also!*
> *Till cruel umbrellas parted the strife (or I might have been choking him yet)*
> *But Thy Servant has had the time of his life – and now shall we call on the vet?'*
>
> R. Kipling

Rommel can be quite fierce and surprisingly frightening. When he's angry not only his hackles but some of the hair along his sides stands erect. The hair on his hindquarters is longer and this makes him look something like a cross between a porcupine and a pangolin.

His lips draw back to reveal remarkably large and well formed teeth and unlike most small dogs he doesn't yap. His bark may not have the resonance of a St Bernard, but it is at least tenor. He has a ferocious base snarl and sounds much larger than he is. All in all he looks and sounds much more impressive than his size warrants.

He also has the unfortunate habit of biting people.

Had he stuck to burglars I would have had no objection, but he was totally indiscriminate in the selection of his victims. This could not only be embarrassing but occasionally placed a heavy load on the bonds of friendship.

In Africa there is a tendency for Africans to tease a dog inside a fence, especially if it barks at them and they feel secure outside. Many years before we had a house in Harare and still had the Alsatians. Molly adored Jean.

One day Jean was gardening by the fence next to the road when an African drove along the road on his bicycle swinging from side to side with carefree joie de vivre. One swing coincided with the patch Jean was working on. Molly under the impression he was about to attack Jean leapt at the fence, the cyclist got such a fright that he promptly fell off.

Later that day we got a note from one of our new neighbours asking if our dogs were going to savage their gardener every time he rode past. They said that this would be inconvenient as he had to pass that way to the bakery to collect their daily bread. As a postscript she asked whether they also savaged small children.

As Molly hadn't touched him and as they had no young children the note erased any sympathy I might have felt, I replied briefly that hopefully it would not occur again, and yes, they did savage small children which was why we only had two left!

The incident didn't end there (even if neighbourly relations did). Two days later Jean heard Molly going wild at the gate, she went out to find the same man cowering on the far side of the road. It turned out that he had been throwing stones at her, then when she had run towards him he had forgotten he was safe outside and in panic had thrown the only other things he had in his hand – the bread money! This was now scattered in our drive beyond his reach, thereafter I think he took a different route to the shops.

I always think that Alsatians must be one of the most maligned breeds around. One is always hearing second and third hand stories about their viciousness. In fact I have never come across one which was properly looked after and cared for that wasn't as gentle as a child. I expect there are rogues, but the only dangerous ones I have known have been maltreated or received no attention and been left tied up for hours on end. Alsatians are the smartest of dogs and can think, and need mental as well as physical activity.

There are also good Alsatian stories and we had one. Sarah at about this time was some four months old and a difficult child. She never slept for more than about an hour and half consecutively and woke crying. We had tried everything with no success and Jean with no sleep for months on end was going insane.

I believe that a high proportion of battered babies have intelligent mothers, I now know how it comes about.

Molly adored Sarah as well as Jean. Sarah had been born just after a litter of Molly's puppies had gone to their new homes and I think that she had a feeling that this was a left over one she had overlooked. From the moment that Sarah arrived Molly would lie by her crib, and took an interest in everything that happened to her.

On the day in question Molly was once again lying in the room near the crib, Sarah woke up, began yelling and Jean came through and picked her up. There was no diminution of the noise and Jean's control finally snapped, she turned Sarah over and raised her hand to give her a good whack on the bottom.

Before she could do so Molly came across the room and took her wrist in her mouth, she held it until she felt Jean had recovered control and then let go and went quietly and lay down again.

Jean was terrified; she said it felt like hours although it was probably only a few seconds. She was so gentle that she hadn't left a mark when she let go. It was an extraordinary action requiring intelligence, reasoning and understanding of Jean's emotional state and intentions.

Happily Sarah improved shortly afterwards and Jean was never driven to the edge of control again.

Many Africans are of course excellent with dogs and every employee I have ever had has been marvellous with ours. The best example was my batman when I was young, carefree and single. He was about my age and what in those days could only be described as a 'wide boy'.

His name was Adam.

Saturday nights he would dress up in skin tight purple pants, shiny patent leather shoes, a brilliant shirt and even louder jacket of contrasting colours, and head for the fleshpots of the town.

I only had Zeus in those days and he adored Zeus and Zeus adored him. If I was going out that evening and couldn't take Zeus he would often ask my permission to take him himself. Off he would swagger with this huge dog at his heels and doubtless made an enormous impression and cut a swathe through the local girls. I knew he would look after him with total care.

Zeus rated far above me in his estimation. Not infrequently Adam would get drunk and return home in in a rollicking humour, barely able to stand.

"Sorry Ishe" he would slur out with a grin "am too drunk to cook your supper but have fed Zeus."

Alas poor Adam – he didn't survive my marriage and a woman in charge and had to part company from me.

Whilst my Alsatians never bit anyone and never even went for anyone unless heavily provoked, Rommel had no discrimination. In general he opposed entry to the premises by anyone outside the family and he bit without provocation and without regard to race, colour, creed or age.

Unfortunately it was almost impossible to know in advance when he was going to take umbrage as he also bit without any warning which made it even harder to guess when he was going to. When his hackles were up and he was snarling or barking he didn't bite. For the purpose of a bite he favoured the silent stealthy approach.

Once the visitor was inside the gate he would stop barking and stalk quietly up the drive at their heels with his head near the ground (not that it was far off normally), closer and closer until his teeth went snap into your ankle. With men in long trousers this usually didn't cause much damage, Rommel being unable to distinguish which was trouser and which was the visitor. With others it could be a painful experience, the fourteen year old son of a friend got bitten to the bone.

He has improved with age and at least twice saved us from serious thefts.

The first occasion was just outside Lusaka, the capital of Zambia. We were returning from a holiday in Malawi when a jagged piece of metal on the road sliced a rear tyre open.

Zambia, and Lusaka in particular, was at that time one of the most lawless places you could come across. People didn't just security-fence and burglar-bar their properties, they also put a double steel door on the bedrooms. When you heard someone smashing their way in and removing the TVs, computers etc., you stayed quiet behind your door. Most people probably had a pistol or a shotgun but the thieves were invariably armed with fully automatic weapons – and didn't hesitate to use them.

However, on this occasion it was still full daylight and we were on an empty stretch of road (or the stretch of foot deep potholes which passed in Zambia for a metalled road) with open farmland on each side and no-one in sight. Jean sat in the cab whilst I got down to the business of changing the wheel. I had nearly finished when a young African man stopped beside me and asked if he could help. I declined and he walked on down the road.

I finished the job and stood up. The man was about thirty yards away now and walking away from us so I called Jean to come round the back of the pick-up and pour some water so I could wash my hands and clean up. She asked if she should lock the cab but as there was still only the one man in sight, and he was some way off and going, I said not to bother.

She came round and I began washing my hands, bent over slightly so that the canopied rear of the truck cut off my view to the front.

Suddenly we heard the dogs going mad in the front and obviously out of the cab. I tore round to find my young friend doing a sort of new variation on a tribal dance. This involved leaping up and down in the air on the spot and howling.

Rommel, underneath, was vainly trying to catch his ankles each time he landed, but was a bit slow and couldn't match the height he was leaping. Fenella was tearing round both in rings giving him vociferous encouragement.

He had been surreptitiously watching us the whole time, and the second we were out of sight at the back, had immediately run back and quietly opened the passenger side door with the idea of snatching whatever was available. My bag was on the seat with our passports, money and all our documents. It was Saturday afternoon and had they been stolen we would have been in serious difficulties when we got to the Zimbabwe/Zambian border.

Rommel inside was, of course, invisible to an outsider's casual glance as he would have been lying down on the seat. For once crime didn't pay – our friend must have got a nasty fright, no doubt he would have been bent double when he opened the door with his head on seat level and the dogs must have gone for him instantaneously..

When I appeared he gave up trying to out leap Rommel and headed for the farmland pursued by the dogs, unfortunately this was bounded by a barb wire fence and in his unseemly haste he left most of his trousers (and hopefully some of him) on it. He did not have a successful afternoon.

The second occasion occurred a few years later when we were living in Malawi. Our house was fenced but not too securely. At the time we had moved there Malawi lived under what could only be described as a mildly benevolent dictatorship. One of the advantages of this was that things like the police actually functioned and generally it was one of the safest and most law abiding countries we had lived in.

Not long after we moved there the Iron Curtain fell and Western donor nations turned their attention elsewhere. Aid was withdrawn from Malawi, the World Bank imposed one of their famous austerity packages, multi-party democracy was demanded by outside nations together with various political conditions.

Malawi complied with the demands but this was apparently not sufficient to get aid restored. Since the country is almost totally aid dependent and very poor, the economic collapse this brought on combined with political chaos brought predictable results, not that this was of any concern to the Governments thousands of miles away who had caused it.

Law and order collapsed, inflation became horrific (a hamburger went from six kwacha to forty-six kwacha in a couple of months) people already poor were deprived of the little that kept them going and began to starve and the apparent licence to now do as you pleased as understood from Western liberal thinking became crime on an unprecedented scale.

Whilst this has nothing do with dachshunds, I could wish that World Bank officials actually had to stay in the counties they prescribe for. The Malawi local representative, residing in an exclusive and expensive suburb and spending a large proportion of each day on the golf course, barely knew what country he was in. There is, no doubt, enormous moral satisfaction in knowing you have prescribed the right medicine, especially when you can distance yourself comfortably from the patent and don't have to watch his subsequent demise at first hand.

At this time the collapse had only just begun and we hadn't yet erected all the bared wire, razor wire and glass wall topping which soon became necessary.

I played duplicate bridge, however, in the interests of matrimonial felicity, I played with another partner than my wife. On this night I was out at bridge and Jean was in the bedroom preparing to go to bed, when she heard a yell of anguish from outside her window followed by a thump and a cry from Rommel.

An intruder had scaled the fence and was standing outside the window trying to look in, doubtless with a view to seeing who was there and what could be stolen – when Rommel came upon him.

Rommel at night was in the habit of patrolling the house and often spent much of the night padding round and round it – this time it paid off.

Both dogs could come and go as they pleased at any time as I had installed a dachshund flap in the front door!

Intent on his fell purpose the unwanted guest obviously didn't hear him coming, and from the yell he must have got a good bite of intruder as opposed to trousers, he tried to attack him again and had received a foot in the stomach for his pains – but the intruder fled empty handed.

In Malawi we lived in a house sited on an eighteen hole golf course in the centre of the capital city, Lilongwe. Whilst I couldn't take the dogs to work with me, it did mean that I could, and did, take them for a comfortable four kilometre walk round the course in the early mornings. At that time the course was usually empty of people, but a plethora of homeless mongrels roamed it, hunted and slept there.

Up until now Rommel had escaped being bitten by a larger dog and still suffered under the impression that they were all terrified of him. Disillusion was in store. One morning he came across a large mongrel and ignoring my commands headed for it and his accustomed moral victory.

Alas this one was not impressed and didn't flee.

As he got close his determination did waiver a little when it failed to exhibit the normal fear and trepidation induced by his approach. He slowed down and closed in at a slower pace. The growls became a mite half hearted. He had a sniff and then decided that it was time it was taught a lesson – and bit one leg – the only part he could reach.

To his amazement instead of running off with its tail between its legs, it took exception to this treatment and not only snarled back but actually bit him. I arrived breathlessly, the mongrel fled and I examined a distraught Rommel. He had a couple of nasty punctures in the chest but nothing too serious. I carried him home for first aid.

He took the lesson to heart. If Jean or I were actually on hand he would still attack, but further from us and on the golf course he adopted a new approach.

Seeing a dog thirty or forty yards off he would run firmly on a straight line which bisected our path and a direct line to the dog. This would be a medium speed effort and whilst he ran he kept his head firmly pointed straight ahead. Never by one twitch would he acknowledge that he had seen the other dog.

"I'm just having a look over here to see if there's anything interesting about." his attitude said.

If the other dog remained in place he would continue past it without a sign that he had noticed it, then veer back onto our path, "Nothing of interest there" he muttered as he rejoined me.

But – let the other dog turn tail or start to move away and in an instant he would be transformed into a demoniacal fury, hackles up, growling ferociously and off after it as fast as his stubby legs would go. As there are few if any, other breeds that Rommel can keep in sight on a chase, this would be brief.

This procedure kept his honour, pride and skin happily intact.

It wasn't long before the dogs discovered that the golf course yielded another very satisfactory prey.

Hedgehogs.

They are common enough in Africa but the dogs had never come across them and oddly enough neither had I. They were a satisfactory prey for a number of reasons. From the dogs point of view they were exciting things to hunt because they lived in shallow holes or under logs, which meant the dogs could indulge in their favourite pastime of digging. From my point of view it was harmless pastime because the dachsies never having read Kipling could find no way to uncurl them no matter how hard they growled and worried at them.

The golf course was home to literally hundreds, and as obviously no-one had ever disturbed them before, they provided an interesting lesson regarding the efficiency of animal information dissemination systems.

I don't know which dachsie was responsible for discovering the first, but Rommel appeared one morning heading for home with a small hedgehog in his mouth.

Fenella was the keenest hunter, but would never have made a suffragette. She is feminine to the core and not a feminist. Women, she consider, are there to be loved, cuddled, coddled and to use their brains to get men to do as they wish them to.

She searches ahead of Rommel and I, and when she finds something gives tongue. This excites Rommel enough to hurry there to join in. On his arrival she withdraws a discreet distance after having indicated the relevant hole (or whatever it is) to him, and remains nearby encouraging him verbally. Rommel is then expected to get on with the hard digging. If he flags she will shoulder him aside for an instant and dig furiously for a few seconds just to show him how it should be done.

She soon learnt that rolled up hedgehogs were prickly and once the unfortunate animal had been unearthed would content herself with the odd bark – the hunt and not the kill was her interest. Rommel never gave up hope. He **KNEW** there was an edible animal inside those prickles! He usually got a sore mouth and little joy. Failing all else he would then pick them up and carry them home where he presumably felt he would be able to deal with them at his leisure.

The hedgehogs didn't appear to suffer any great psychological damage. Put them down and within a few moments they would uncurl and wander slowly away. The dogs never hurt one although once it was a close run thing. They dug up a mother and (presumably) father and a collection of babies – a prickle of hedgehogs? In the excitement of finding two large hedgehogs together at once the dogs either didn't notice or didn't recognise the babies who were scattered all over the place. Neither for a moment, did I.

They were about an inch long and too young to curl up. They lay flat, looking rather like miniature starfish or minute animal skins stretched out on the hearth, each was covered with tiny soft bristles. I drove the dogs off and restored them to their home.

The golf course covered an area of about one hundred and fifteen hectares, between the fairways there were numerous copses and natural pieces of land, and along one side there was a river. It was near the centre of the old town and the area surrounding it was all built up. Until the dachsies began hunting them, the hedgehogs had obviously never been bothered by predators, and it hadn't been necessary to ensure that your house was burglar proof.

They lived in shallow holes, under light pieces of wood or even sometimes simply under a layer of dead leaves.

It took every hedgehog on the course just three months to get the message, after that time the dogs rarely ever caught another one, each was securely ensconced in a deep safe hole or in a dachsie proof place. The dogs knew where they were but they couldn't get at them. The only ones they ever caught thereafter were small and young and had evidently failed to heed parental advice.

I have no idea how hedgehogs communicate, but the change was so universal that I am convinced the message was somehow passed around. Hedgehog communications are obviously far more sophisticated than I had realised.

When you are a miniature dachshund and weigh ten pounds, it is not easy to find suitable prey to hunt, it's more a case of things hunting you!

Lizards are their preferred prey (although they don't taste too nice!), but snakes look much like lizards – and we worried about them getting bitten.

My sister, Lyn, lives in Tanzania and had a pack of Jack Russells. They are plagued with big cobras and year after year the dogs killed a succession of these in the garden. Every year she also lost a number of dogs who got bitten in the process.

Before Bruno fought Tyson for the second time I remember hearing Henry Cooper on the radio saying that what Bruno lacked was a sense of self preservation and because of this he would lose. He did of course. Jack Russells' obviously have the same problem.

The dachsies on the other hand, have one. Something which seems to me a sign of remarkable good sense. Fen, early on in Kariba found a small spitting cobra in a pipe. The pipe was just large enough to admit her nose but fortunately not her eyes. She got a load of venom on her nose but suffered no ill effects. This did at least persuade her that snakes should be treated with caution. After that if they found one they circled it warily giving tongue until help arrived. It was just as well, as on one occasion they found an eight foot cobra (the biting kind) had they tried to attack it it would almost certainly have killed them both.

We also found out at Kariba how much venom a big spitting cobra has. Our washing line was at the side of the house near a six foot security fence which was heavily covered with a thick creeper. Hanging up washing one day Jean disturbed a big cobra which spat at her. She got a fair amount on her face but luckily she wears glasses and these protected her eyes. We never saw any sign of the snake but when I went out there were blobs of venom looking like white foam, the size of my fist, still hanging on the leaves.

The other favourite prey was naturally mice. In Kariba they were rarely seen, if you were a mouse in Kariba you were at the bottom of the food chain and you needed caution to survive – there were so many things after you. In Lilongwe, Malawi, life was better mouse wise.

You can do things with small dogs which you can't with big ones – there was no reason in Lilongwe that they couldn't go out at night on their own, so as I mentioned we had cut a dachsie flap in the front door. It turned out to have a disadvantage I hadn't considered – it not only let dachsies out but let mice in.

I am all in favour of living and letting live, but mice in the house are really not tolerable. They invariably take up residence in the stove or fridge where in due course they turn all the electrical insulation into nests and eat the wire.

Mice drive dachsies mad, they are one prey that Fenella feels women should take the lead in catching. Lizards are fun, hedgehogs OK – but mice are the best – and edible. She caught one once when we weren't looking and swallowed it whole like a mongoose with a snake. When we found her, the tip of the tail was just disappearing down her gullet.

Rommel's heart is in mouse hunting but speed and agility are not his strong points, and although I hate to say it most mice can out think him. Rommel takes time to ponder alternatives. If the mouse was once seen at point A, then he expects it to remain there until he can catch it. It is unthinkable that it should remove itself to point B without his permission.

This usually means that where Rommel is – the mouse is not!

One day we definitely had a mouse, it had been spotted and was in the lounge. We had a big solid backed bookcase against one wall and the dachsies were going mad at it. I moved one end out from the wall and Rommel who happened to be at that end shot in behind it.

I looked over the back. The bookcase was now diagonal to the wall and Rommel had got in as far as he could until his shoulders became jammed between the back of the bookcase and the wall.

He could see there was no mouse in front of him but the scent was there, at first I didn't see the mouse either.

By Rommel's shoulders and just above him there was an electric wall plug with a 13 amp socket plugged in to it. The mouse had its front feet on this and its back feet braced against the bookcase, like a mountaineer in a chimney. Meanwhile it straddled Rommel's back.

Efforts to distract Rommel's attention from the vacant smelly space in front of him to the mouse poised two inches above his back failed. The mouse deciding it had been observed, let go, jumped on Rommel's back, ran along to his tail, jumped onto the floor and made its escape through the dachsie flap not to be seen again.

He has killed some, but these successes have usually arisen when the mouse fleeing happens to pass right in front of his nose enabling him to have one quick snap. Jean says Fen misses as many as Rommel but this statement is, I fear, based more on support for Rommel than on the facts.

An unending stream appeared to come through the flap. The trouble was knowing whether they were still inside or had left after a quick look around. The dogs would come back, smell a mouse and go berserk. On one occasion Fen pulled a whole row of large encyclopaedias off a book shelf under the erroneous impression that they were harbouring a mouse.

Usually she was right and eventually we would dislodge it from whatever haven it had found in the back of the stove or the freezer. If she lost interest after a few hours it could be assumed that the mouse had left.

Rommel is, I have to admit, not the only one who suffers from the delusion that prey once seen at point A will forever remain there. Fenella does with lizards. At the Yacht Club in Kariba there were always small boats lying on the hard, right way up or upside down, invariably there were lizards sheltering under them.

Fenella, discovering this early in life drew the obvious conclusion. Boats harboured lizards. It was dachsies job in life to flush them out and catch them. A lack of success in such places as Belgium in early spring and Turkey in midwinter has not yet succeeded in disillusioning her.

Dachsies were, I am told, originally used as badger hunting dogs (standard size ones that is). They are certainly left with a desire to go down any holes they can find. We have always had nightmares that one day one will get stuck somewhere where we can't get at it. Rommel in particular is liable to get stuck, I once had to dig up twenty yards of a drain beside a swimming pool to recover him. Fortunately he does know his limitations and is relatively cautious, this is just as well as being the strong silent type he disdains to call for help and waits in silence to be rescued, thus making it difficult to know where he is.

Fenella on the other hand can get in and out of a tube the size of her body. She has only got stuck once. She went down a drain (also beside a swimming pool). This emerged some thirty yards away from the pool but was clogged up at the outlet. Finding herself about a foot from daylight and unable to dig or push her way out she took action.

She makes her wishes known verbally, whether it is something she wants or whether it is merely that she feels excluded from the conversation and wishes to join in. The first request is made quite politely but unless a response is forthcoming immediately the volume increases dramatically.

I heard a subterranean yelp which rapidly increased in volume and frequency, however, once we had tracked her down and got picks and started working to lift the slab at the end she stopped, presumably confident that all was now well in hand. When we did raise it we found her comfortably curled up awaiting rescue, she could no doubt have gone back by the way she had come – but why do so when an instruction to the labouring classes will get you out without any further effort?

Fenella's besetting sin is, like most women, jealousy. All dogs are jealous but Fenella objects strongly to me interacting closely with anyone, person or dog.

I am allowed to love Rommel but in very limited doses – say about five seconds at a time. At first she would leap down and insert herself between the two of us and make a big fuss of Rommel to distract his attention from me. Then she worked out a cunning ploy.

Once she thought Rommel had had as much of my attention as he was due (five seconds) she would leap off her chair and tear out of the door barking furiously. Rommel naturally assumed that something interesting was going on and would rush after her adding his mite. The minute he was out of the house Fenella would return quietly and come over to me looking pleased with herself.

"That's disposed of him" she would say "Just you remember I'm the only one in your life."

Poor Rommel would remain vainly tearing around outside growling fiercely and looking for the non-existent enemy. He never figured it out and the ploy worked every time.

About this time, Rommel, who was now eight years old, began to cause problems. I have a feeling it is quite common in dachsie dogs. He was alright with me but on a number of occasions he turned on Fenella viciously and without reason. The attacks were unprovoked and did not involve actual violence, but it was obviously only a matter of time before he hurt her.

We discussed it with our vet and reluctantly decided that we had no choice but to have him castrated. We did and the attacks ceased, unfortunately as a consequence he became even stouter and it had no effect on his desire to kill other dogs.

Nine months after this we nearly lost him. He got the equivalent of acute appendicitis. Naturally there was nowhere in Malawi where we could get him X-rayed and as a result we waited until the situation was desperate before letting him have exploratory surgery. It turned out to be a major operation on his insides but he recovered well.

Then only three months later he exhibited the same symptoms again. This time it turned out to be a twisted intestine and another major operation. The trauma of this second operation so soon after the first was almost too much for him. For eight days he hovered between life and death with daily visits from the vet.

At the end of this period not only Rommel, but Jean was in a state of collapse and we were seriously considering putting him down to stop his misery. I began to feel that the kindest thing was to do the same to Jean and started looking for a suitably venal doctor, euthanasia not being on the Malawi statute books!

On the eighth day the vet looked at Rommel and looked at Jean.

"If he was going to die from complications" he said "Then it would have happened by now. I think the problem is mental. "You." he said to Jean "are communicating your distress to him and this is stopping him from making the mental effort to get better. I want you to stay as faraway from him as possible, stop feeling sorry for him, and talk to him bracingly"

I might add that Jean had spent most of the time on a mattress on the floor to be with him as we dared not put him on anything which he might fall off or try and jump off.

We didn't stay away from him but we did try and be bracing and matter of fact as if nothing was wrong. It worked. Within twenty-four hours he had started to move around and within forty-eight he was visibly on the road to recovery. Well done Tony Ndovi!

The problem has never returned, not that poor Rommel is limited to stomach ailments, he is also prone to tonsillitis, but at least we can recognise that and a course of antibiotics quickly rectifies the situation.

Fenella thank goodness is hardly ever sick and apart from her motorcycle accident and until much later she swallowed a fishhook, line and sinker in the Greek islands near Corfu, I can't remember a day when she was off colour.

Chapter Six

"You have heard the call of the offshore wind,
And the voice of the deep sea rain,
You have heard the song – how long? How long?
Pull out on the trail again."

R. Kipling

1994 was not a happy year.

It began with Rommel's operations and ended with me resigning my job as the culmination of a number of factors.

Aid to Malawi had been withdrawn, inflation was rampant, the amount we were saving had dropped by two thirds. In the new Western ordered democracy law and order had collapsed and as usual in Africa concurrent with the other problems racialism had reared its ugly head.

On top of this I loathed my job which had given me a minor ulcer and two attacks of diabetes in the previous year. Sensibly we should have gone back to Zimbabwe and either looked for another job or invested our limited savings in a small business.

We did neither. Jean, whose family goes back three hundred years in Africa had had enough of it – the racialism, corruption, mismanagement, politics and always having to watch ever word you said.

England was out because at that time the ridiculous and cruel quarantine laws meant six months locked up for the dogs. The only people at that time who benefited were the owners of the quarantine kennels who were probably the biggest supporters at the time of the Tory party.

How dangerous the legislation of that time was, was brought home to us on many occasions later when we kept meeting people in Europe with their pets. Asked how they got them in and out, most said casually that they simply put them out of sight and drove home. God knows how many people in boats crossing the channel in summer picked up stray puppies etc. and brought them back. Every time meant a risk of the import of rabies. At least today with the microchips and passports people (including us) can take their pets in and out and it is worth getting the proper papers to do so and thus obviating the risk of importing a truly terrible disease.

I have always loved boats; Jean on the other hand is terrified of sailing and not too enamoured of boats which she distrusts. I had built my first one out of old paraffin cans in central Tanganyika when I was fourteen, had since built a number of others ranging from dinghies to a thirty foot offshore yacht which had taken me ten years to build in my back yard. The latter we had intended to take to sea, however, by the time I finished it, the Rhodesian war and sanctions were in full swing and although I could have taken her out of the country we would not have been able to take any money out at all with which to finish her on the coast; so we sold her and bought a little eighteen footer for use on the lakes at home.

If we left Malawi and we wanted to do something different it was now or never. The children were grown up and married, we had no responsibility except to ourselves and if we left it any later we would probably be too old and cautious.

"Anything's better than this" said Jean "Alright lets buy a boat outside and go somewhere new."

Also for the first time we had a little money saved in a usable currency as we had been able to remit some of our salary from Malawi. In Rhodesia in those days it was impossible to take money out or change it in anything but minute quantities (the holiday allowance for a family for a year was the equivalent of some £ 200!) and the black market was simply too expensive.

We didn't have enough money for even an old boat large enough for ocean cruises (we did require some comfort in our mid fifties) but we did have enough for a small second hand one.

Many years previously I had come across a sort of autobiography called 'The Way of a Transgressor' by an American Negley Farson. I thought then, and still think, that it was a work that far transcended any fiction you could imagine, he had had an extraordinary life. One of the chapters concerned a trip that he and his wife had made across Europe from the North Sea to the Black sea via canals and rivers, in a little twenty six foot yacht.

At the time I had read it, it had caught my imagination, however, he had made the trip in 1925 on the old Ludwig canal which linked the river Main to the Danube and thus East and West Europe, and this was, to all intents and purposes, barely navigable even then.

I had never heard anything else about it and assumed that if it was disused in 1925 it would have been closed years ago, then one evening friends of ours Bob and Claire Medland came round for dinner. For some reason I was talking about Farson and his book and mentioned his trip across Europe.

Bob who is a mine of usually useless statistics said "I'm sure I've seen something about a Danube canal somewhere recently, I think it was in National Geographic."

The next day he dropped off the magazine and sure enough there was a long article about a new East/West canal.

It is a fascinating story. It is only a short distance (a little over one hundred kilometres) over the continental divide separating the headwaters of the River Main from the Danube, one flowing West and one East. The Danube has always been a route into central Europe and the first attempt to link the two sides was made in the 8th century by Charlemagne who threw a horde of labourers in to dig a canal. This unfortunately filled with mud and water after heavy rains and he gave up the attempt, although I believe some of it can still be seen.

Then in the early nineteenth century Ludwig of Bavaria actually built a canal. Unfortunately this was too small to be commercially viable (it resembled the English narrow canals of today) and in fact Ludwig never even bothered to attend its opening. It also had a problem in that seasonal fluctuations in the level of the Main made that river unnavigable at times, so it was never a commercial success.

It was the remains of this clogged canal that Farson had used.

Then at the beginning of the twentieth century a company was formed in Germany and a new canal was begun. This was a huge undertaking involving locking and making navigable the Main as well as the upper Danube, each lock became a small hydro electric station to help pay for the construction and financial help given by various provincial Governments in Southern Germany. Construction went on for over seventy years (with a few pauses for World Wars one and two) until it was finally completed in 1994.

The canal passes down the Altmuhl valley in Bavaria, which is one of the great unspoilt natural beauty spots of Germany. The howls of protest meant that finally some thirty percent of the total cost of the canal was spent on the environment to make it look as natural as possible and to provide breeding grounds and backwaters for wildfowl.

Jean's unexpected volte-face with regard to my boating mania was very welcome, but the more I thought about it the more impractical the scheme seemed. We had very little money and no external income and even an old boat would leave us nothing to live on. Then as I went to bed that night it came to me in a blinding flash – perhaps we could also cross Europe via the new Main/Danube canal.

To make the crossing we wouldn't need a large boat, it would have to be seaworthy, and a yacht, so that we could sail out of the Black Sea and get down to the Mediterranean, but we could coast hop down there and wouldn't need something which carried large quantities of water and provisions. Jean would be much happier starting on the waterways with land on both sides and we could probably just afford to do it.

Finally of course, as it would be though Europe there would be no problem taking the dachsies.

The war in Yugoslavia meant that up to now no-one would have been able to make the entire journey from sea to sea so there was the added bonus that we would almost certainly be the first or amongst the first, people to do so for over seventy years.

We made up our minds that night, wrote off to the canal company and various embassies, scrounged a 'Teach yourself German' tape from the very helpful local embassy and sent off letters to every yacht broker in England and Holland whose address we could find.

Within a surprisingly short space of time we had enough information to know it was at least feasible. I put in my notice, we booked air tickets all round Southern Africa and to England (we felt we had better pay our last respects to our children and Jean wanted to see her sisters and her mother) and began the alarming process of selling everything we possessed that wouldn't fit in two suitcases.

It was a traumatic time added to by Jean unexpectedly having to go to Zimbabwe for a major operation at a moments notice, and the fact that we would have to leave the dogs in kennels until we could get ourselves (and hopefully a boat) to Europe. On top of this my diabetes raised its head again and I felt thoroughly unwell.

The worst thing about leaving the dogs was that we had no idea how long it would be before we could get them back, but there was no choice, so into kennels they went in Malawi. Rommel as usual was busy hurling imprecations at the next door neighbours, but when I got to the end of the run and said to Fenella 'Stay', she sunk to the ground in abject misery and her look haunted me the whole time I was away from her.

Buying a boat in a strange country, then checking and equipping it, especially when you're not sure exactly what you'll need and when every penny counts, is not a simple business. Particularly when you have no transport to get around with.

Miracles do happen. Naturally most of the yacht brokers had sent me details of boats which bore little or no relation to the specifications I had asked for. It was also becoming apparent to me that I needed to alter these anyway. I had been in England about ten days was sitting surrounded by dozens of advertisements for yachts, when Claire Medland phoned me. They had moved back to England six months before and were living some sixty miles away; she was not working and was bored.

"Come and have lunch" she said "I'll drive over and pick you up".

There were a few boats on my list in the immediate area including one at Lyme Regis, only forty minutes drive away. In fact I had decided that she wouldn't suit and wasn't going to look at her, but Claire's arrival coupled with wheels seemed too good an opportunity to miss. When she arrived I broke the glad news that I would buy her a pub lunch but in the meanwhile we were going on a long tour of boats for sale. After all it was their fault that I was there and boat hunting in the first place!

A week later I had bought Rainbow and I still owe Claire a debt of gratitude, without her I would probably never have even looked at her.

She was fifteen years old, twenty-six foot long and there was a lot to be done to her. Jean joined me a week later after visiting her mother in Cape Town, and we got down to serious outfitting. Rainbow was put in the water in April and we finally got aboard and with much trepidation set off up the channel, our main objective being to get to the continent as soon as possible and arrange to have the dachsies flown over.

KLM flew direct from Lilongwe to Amsterdam and we planned to fly the dogs as soon as we could get there. Originally our plan had been to go up the Rhine through Holland, however stories about Dutch officiousness and requirements for certificates (of which we had none) put me off and then it became apparent to me that we were not powerful or fast enough to go up the Rhine against the current anyway. As you will have noticed our plans had a grand idea but we lacked much information as to detail!

We got as far as Ostende in Belgium and decided to enter the canals there, cross Northern France to Strasbourg and then go *down* the Rhine to where we would turn off up the Main. Since our only means of navigation consisted of a large scale waterways map of Europe (stopping at Hungary) and only showing large cities, we seldom knew exactly where we were, where we were going, or how we were going to get there – or if we could –it made life exciting if nothing else!

We phoned friends in Malawi and asked them to get the dogs on a flight. We had checked before leaving that they did take dogs but it now turned out that they only took them if they were accompanied by their owners! As usual we had neglected to check thoroughly enough. However, thank God, for good friends and small countries where everyone knows everyone. Somehow Trev and Jill circumvented the regulations and got them on as special cargo. We hired a small car, and at one in the morning headed for Schipol to meet the flight which arrived at six.

As all the arrangements had to be made from public phones (mobiles were not around) and no-one could contact us directly, communications were a problem. We were both in a state of panic – would the dogs be on the flight, would they be alright, would there be trouble with customs?

Fortunately with our early start the motorways were empty so I managed to cope with a strange car and left hand drive. After forty years of driving a right hand one I kept looking for the rear view mirrors in the wrong places. However, we only had one incident, in Ghent we somehow turned off the motorway and got lost. At last we found two men in the deserted town. Despite the language problem, both were extremely helpful and indeed happy. After twenty minutes we left them arguing vociferously with each other over the best way and pointing in opposite directions. Finally I flagged a car down who helpfully set us on our way again and at 4.30am we were in Schipol.

I don't wish to be rude about Schipol but I always understood it was a major international airport. In actual fact it closed down at night apart from the odd small café. There were no staff, information desks were unmanned and nowhere you could get any information at all.

As 6am approached we were getting desperate. We finally found the correct entry gate but as the dachsies were hardly likely to get off and emerge with the passengers, it didn't help. At last just after six and after the flight had landed, a few sleepy, disgruntled and unhelpful KLM staff came on duty. Fifteen minutes later we finally found a man who was prepared to help. He phoned around and yes – another miracle –the dogs were on board, but we had to collect them from the animal hospital a mile away.

Off we set and someone was actually on duty there – BUT – first we must go to another block and clear the customs papers. We went. Naturally customs didn't come on duty until 7.30am!

At last, lighter in the pocket and laden with sheaves of stamped documents we returned to the animal hospital. All was in order, they said, go outside and they would bring the dogs. We went and a man appeared with two small wooden kennels.

"Fenella" I said tentatively and thought there was a small muffled response. What I wondered, had happened to Murphy's law? It seemed too good to be true – what if they were the wrong dogs, what if ours had been sent to somewhere like Afghanistan in error? Baggage doesn't matter when - as frequently occurs this happens – but dogs!

The man opened the kennels one at a time. I don't know if they really check but I got the impression that if a dog emerged and didn't recognise the person waiting for it then there would be some difficult questions to answer!

Into a cold watery dawn of weak spring sunshine emerged Rommel, bounded at me and then leapt into Jean's arms. Fen came out, a small back bullet, all over me, then Jean, then round and round in circles of displacement activity. Back to me and sure at last that we were there, her curiosity at this strange place took over

"Be there lizards here" you could hear her ask herself – and off quickly with Rommel to have a look.

I don't know about Jean, but I had forgotten how small they were. Living with them everyday you became used to it and thinking of Fenella as slim and Rommel as, well …well…well… well set up! In that instant when they came out they both simply looked tiny. They were both in excellent condition and both had lost some weight, Rommel for once looked quite svelte.

We gave them both a drink, a small snack, piled them into the car and back to Belgium.

The spring of 1995 was not a pleasant one and it seemed forever until summer arrived, but we were at least blessed with reasonable weather that day. The sun shone though what the dachsies thought of the temperature I have no idea.

Before we left Malawi Jean had made them both felt lined jackets. To avoid losing them, and because I have a predilection for it, these were bright orange. Jilly King, our friend in Malawi who had despatched them, had a sister who did fancy embroidery and whilst they were in the kennels she had very sweetly emblazoned their names on each jacket in large script, each letter in a different and, if possible, more startling colour.

They were wearing their coats when they arrived and resembled more than anything else a kind of brilliantly coloured tropical armadillo. The coats certainly served their purpose, not only did they keep them warm, but one glimpse of them in the distance and they stood out like a flash of sun.

It was just as well they had them, by that evening it was blowing a force 8 gale in Ostende with driving rain and bitterly cold. The evening's widdle break was unpleasing for all of us. Neither of them had ever come across temperatures even similar. I don't know what Rommel thought, but Fen who considers 25C to be Arctic didn't approve.

Rainbow has no heater and the grill on the stove doubles for this purpose. Unfortunately the boat designers never considered this alternative use and set the stove at waist height. It heated our small home very quickly – but in layers. If you stood up in the cabin from your waist to your head you were as warm as toast, from your waist to your knees you were comfortably warm and from the knees down it was distinctly chilly.

The seat level falls between the distinctly chilly and not too bad levels. In a space craft where the dachsies could have floated against the ceiling they would have been fine, but on our seats they had to be kept wrapped in layers of sleeping bags and spare jerseys.

We quickly found there were two problems with dogs on a boat.

It is amazing how much muck you can get into a boat even if you religiously remove your shoes every time you come aboard. Our first two months were not only cold but very wet. Dachsies are designed with low tummy clearances (ours with about one inch), this means that not only their paws get muddy but their undersides as well. No matter how well you towelled them dry on their re-entry, damp mud, earth, moulted dog hairs and damp dog smell became the hall marks of Rainbow's interior.

The second problem was the toilet facilities. On those intrepid boats going for months without the sight of land the dogs presumably learn or bust! We are in general land-hoppers, this suits Jean better and she ruthlessly used the dogs as an excuse not to stay away from it for too long. Still there were longish periods when they couldn't go ashore.

We tried to train them. We heard somewhere that traditionally a piece of rope soaked with urine was used – nonsense! We tried a sort of cat's box, then we tried newspaper. This was all very wearing. First you had to take them ashore with the chosen material, then you trailed after them holding it and watching like a hawk so that when they did have a widdle you could dip it in for the smell.

With the newspaper there was a particular problem, because we saved it on the boat where it was always useful, we could never remember which piece was which and I never fancied draining my chips on the wrong piece.

Naturally they were both housetrained, but there have been occasions to our extreme embarrassment where they have been taken into a friend's house, had a quick sniff, found something irresistible and promptly had a wee on the carpet or walls.

BUT – go to the toilet on Rainbow – their home – NEVER.

We spent fruitless hours with them on the foredeck and on one long trip Fenella finally got the message, but she only did that once. Rommel would rather have died.

Rommel is the only dog I have ever come across who is embarrassed by his toilet needs. You don't expect it of dogs who usually have more common sense than us. His problem is that he is so solid his back doesn't bend too well, when he was younger this failure meant that occasionally you had to wipe his bottom, this caused him great embarrassment and was obviously psychologically damaging as well.

He evolved a new toilet system of his own to avoid it. He finds a rock, a leaf, a branch or even a wall of suitable height, backs up to it and lays his offering gently on it. Against a wall he actually managed to stick it on. What the poor boy needs is a patent dachshund toilet seat but I have never been able to work out a design. I often wonder whether other dogs, or indeed people, are surprised to come across these little sausages carefully deposited on a large leaf six inches from the ground!

Back in Ostende, we took them into town for some last minute shopping, took our mast down and began their triumphant procession across Europe. There was no other word for it.

The English like to consider themselves as the great dog lovers of this world, but we think the accolade should go to Belgium. Never in our lives have we seen so many dogs and of such assorted types, Every Belgian appeared to own at least one adored dog. No particular breed predominated, in fact the majority's parents had obviously indulged in miscegenation on a grand scale down the years.

Smooth haired dachsies are, if not common, at least not rare in Zimbabwe and much the same applies to England. On the continent they appeared to be non existent, in fact the first one we met was twelve months and some twelve countries later on a Greek island in the Aegean Sea.

That one actually saved us a fair amount of money. Water on the Aegean islands is precious, often imported by tanker and when you filled the yacht (all 70 odd litres) you paid. On this occasion the water seller was the owner of the dachsie and so impressed with us having two that he waived all charges with the comment that the water was free for the dogs!

Our first stroll in Ostende gave us an inkling of what was to become a common experience. First their eyes were drawn like magnets to the magnificent orange coats, then they observed the dogs inside. They were a source of absolute amazement. People stopped, people stared, pointed, called acquaintances attention to them, came over and asked us about them and tried to make friends with them.

The dogs were indifferent to this royal progress and not being fluent linguists (us that is) we had to quickly develop an efficient mime to say be careful with them. They are never that enamoured of strangers and I could see us ending up in some dank continental gaol if one of them bit the Chief of Police's pride and heir.

At first they tended to take exception but after a while they became resigned. Whilst not being forthcoming they would stand patiently on street corners whilst men, women and children made cooing noises over them in obscure languages.

The interest level varied a bit but never dropped off, Belgium to Greece they tended to receive much the same treatment. What's more only once did they bite anyone, that was Rommel and it really wasn't his fault.

We were moored in a tiny fishing harbour called Kaynarpinar in the Gulf of Izmir, in Turkey. In fact we stayed there three months and still almost think of it as home. It was winter and the population had shrunk to about seventy people with the close of the tourist season. The one restaurant had closed but the other remained open in a half hearted sort of way. This was run by the son of the owner and not infrequently in the evenings when he closed early through lack of business he would drop by to have a drink with us on Rainbow. His restaurant was just at the end of the quay and only about fifty yards from where we were moored.

On this occasion he arrived a little later than usual and somewhat the worse for wear. Turkish raki being a spirit with which it is not wise to trifle. The freedom to celebrate we understood, being caused by the absence of his wife for a couple of nights, something which he was obviously determined to make the most of!

He sat down and Rommel, who knew him, was on the floor by his feet. Hickmet, himself, owned a large cross Doberman which he was used to knocking around in play. Full of the joie de raki he leant down and did the same to Rommel. Rommel didn't actually bite him, but he snarled a warning to stop before I could intervene. Hickmet got such a fright that he snatched his hand back and in the process got a graze on it from one of Rommel's teeth. It was minute; he had to squeeze it hard to raise a tiny drop of blood. The Turks are like the French, they take an almost morbid interest in their health, also, which we didn't realise, in Turkey they are terrified of rabies.

Never have you heard such a fuss. He called the local vet from a nearby town ten kilometres away (this at 11.30 at night) and I felt it politic to pay the vet's taxi fare, I felt that at any moment we would all find ourselves in a Turkish gaol. I must admit that the whole incident caused us more alarm than it might have because of guilty consciences. We had considerably overstayed our Turkish visa and theoretically were there illegally.

This was my fault as the cost of our visa was considerable and the officialdom involved was debilitating, also there was no way of renewing them where we were, and we would have had to make a thirty kilometre bus trip to Izmir, a big city, and then try and find the various offices involved. Jean being very law abiding, was all for doing this. However it had taken me all day to book us and the boat into Turkey at Istanbul and I pointed out that after all this work and expense no-one in five months had even asked us for any papers. I foresaw no reason why they should now - and said to hell with it!

Fortunately the vet turned out to be a charming man and could even understand and speak a few words of English. The dogs had had all their injections in Turkey only a few weeks before, he examined their Turkish papers briefly and then Hickmet. One glance was enough for him to sum up the situation and he promptly removed his half filled glass and told him to sober up.

Poor Hickmet, by morning he had travelled to the nearest town with a doctor, seen him and got himself at least two injections and about five courses of pills. I gathered (neither of us spoke more than a word or two of each other's language) that he rather hoped I would contribute towards his medical expenses, but by this time I had rather lost interest in his histrionics over a tiny scratch.

It took a couple of weeks to restore amicable relations.

We were undoubtedly lucky though, if you take your dogs to strange places, then you cannot afford to let them bite people, whoever's fault it is. Legally (we discovered later), the vet should have impounded Rommel and kept him in kennels for a full ten days. As it was he merely told us that they must be kept on leads for that period if we took them off the boat.

Germany, though, was the country in which they generated the most interest. Dachshund sounds very Germanic and I had always assumed that it was a German word. Where it comes from I have no idea but to our amazement we found that no German had ever heard of it, they call them 'teckels'.

And teckels there were aplenty in Germany, teckels of every shape, size and hair type, but not one less than three times Fenella's size and for that matter we never saw a smooth haired one.

On nice days the dogs would stand in the cockpit with their feet on the coaming, viewing the passing scenery. People on the shore would look once, look twice and then with great excitement hold up their versions of dachshunds and wave a greeting.

The other thing that caused great excitement in Germany was that there were two of them. We never fathomed out why two should be so much more sensational than one. They would see one, clasp their hands to their chests and exclaim loudly, then the second dog would hove in sight.

"Swie" they would gasp and become almost petrified with wonder.

I have a delightful brother-in-law who is German, but with the Germans who ever really knows what they think, Rommel must have felt at home there.

At least we know now that we have a career to fall back on when all else fails. Begging on a street corner with the two dachsies in Germany, I could make a fortune.

Chapter Seven

"Life's all getting and giving,
I've only myself to give,
What shall I do for a living?
I've only one life to live.
End it? I'll not find another,
Spend it? But how shall I best?
Sure the wise plan is to live like a man,
And Luck may look after the rest!
Largesse, Largess, Fortune!
Give or hold at your will.
If I've no care for Fortune
Fortune must follow me still.'

R. Kipling

With the mast on deck, dogs below, and last minute provisions packed we finally locked out of Ostende harbour in a light drizzle and set off three and a half thousand kilometres across Europe.

We really didn't know what we were doing. That is we knew where we wanted to try and go but didn't really know if it could be done, a new outbreak of war in Yugoslavia would find us stranded half way down the Danube, and even if there wasn't we weren't sure that we could get through. We had no idea what we would do when we finished or even if we had enough money to finish! On top of this we only had the one large scale map of the rivers and canals of Western Europe and hadn't actually decided on a route.

However, the dachsies being back with us our spirits rose noticeably despite early spring weather which seemed Arctic to us, and we all began slowly to adapt to living in a space some nine feet wide and about ten long.

It must have seemed very strange to the dogs. Jean worried about them getting enough exercise and that they would feel 'cabined, cribbed, confined', but in fact I don't think it bothered them at all. Anyway they had just spent nearly three months in kennels which weren't much bigger and were certainly far less interesting, and finally to them, as to us, all that really mattered was that they were with us again.

Fenella, curious as always, enjoyed exploring the nooks and crannies of Rainbow – it was beyond belief that something with so many little dark holes and little cupboards, didn't harbour colonies of lizards and mice. It was a long time before she gave up.

The double V bunk in the forrard cabin was too high for them to jump onto, but they could make it onto the seats. The companionway steps to the cockpit were too steep for them, but by jumping first onto the seat by the navigation table and then from there sideways onto the top step they learnt to get in and out of the cabin on their own.

This at first was a rather perilous undertaking, especially for Rommel. Once the jump had been made onto the top step, actually getting out into the cockpit was a major problem. The step was just wide and long enough for him to stand on it, but then to get into the cockpit he had to turn sideways and climb over the foot high coaming and down the other side into the cockpit itself. This required a degree of agility and suppleness which he lacked and at first there were a number of tragedies when he slipped and fell bumpety bump down onto the lower step and thence onto the cabin floor. With practice he improved and later managed well unless the boat happened to pitch at the fatal moment.

At first though neither was very tempted to climb out at all, a cold grey spring was even less to their liking than ours. Fenella in particular disapproved. She did though, discover some consolation in the duvet.

Duvets are not things in great demand in Central Africa and we had never owned one. Jean (being female) knew about these things and instructed me to buy one for the boat, and like any obedient husband I had obeyed. It was not an easy purchase. I naturally assumed that a duvet was a duvet was a duvet – you went in and bought whichever colour you wanted. Faced, in Argos, with a whole catalogue of different togs I found myself at a loss. My instructions had not mentioned these things. What was a 'tog' anyway? However, after half an hour of indecision and sidling up to motherly looking women and seeking enlightenment, I managed a purchase.

Duvets Fenella decided immediately were perfect Fenella things. Light, soft, warm and ideally suited to a dachsie. In cold weather you could curl up under it and in hot weather it was deliciously soft to sink into from the top. When the weather finally did improve a glance into the cabin would reveal a small black ball comfortably ensconced, looking as one could imagine as did the dormouse in 'Alice'.

In the cold weather, once under it and warm, there was no luring her out. Rommel could be barking furiously in the cabin or cockpit, but she felt emergence was beyond the call of duty. The small hump in the centre would stir and emit the muffled sound of Fenella's contribution – but no Fenella.

Occasionally if she felt that something really exciting was occurring, then a long black nose and two button eyes would issue from under the edge in the doorway and have a look. Unless it was truly an exceptional event these would soon retreat into the warm centre again.

We would take them ashore before breakfast for a short run and toilet break. In that icy spring and at the end of the year in the Turkish winter Fenella soon worked out the best approach. First she would have to be coaxed out from under the duvet and would emerge with considerable reluctance. Once out and you could hear her say

"Oh alright, let's get it over with."

Put ashore she would complete her toilet almost instantaneously and trot straight back to Rainbow and stand shivering pathetically on the quayside until lifted back aboard and re-installed under the duvet.

Rommel's tummy takes longer to work, requires considerable consideration first and needs a bit of exercise, which meant that you had to hang around in the cold and damp, but even he learnt to act promptly when it was exceptionally unpleasant.

Fenella and I settled in pretty quickly, Jean and Rommel took longer, especially Rommel. It was all nerve wracking what with the wind and the rain drumming on the deck above and not infrequently that great dog in the sky could be heard having a go at him.

Rommel loves Jean, however, perhaps because she is a female he has limited faith in her as a protector. In this is he mistaken as she would probably defend him with her life, whilst under extreme pressure I might just possibly abandon him. In minor crises he seeks Jean, when major troubles beset him, such as that great dog in the sky he feels the need of a more substantial guardian and seeks me.

On a boat this is sometimes extremely inconvenient as protection means, if not actually being on your lap, being as close to you and touching you in as many places as possible.

He was also alarmed to find himself surrounded by that wet and insubstantial substance, water. If that wasn't bad enough there was the fact that in the canals the land was only a matter of a few yards away on each side.

Rainbow's cockpit is almost perfect for dachsies, it's quite deep with high sides which are low enough for the dogs to stand on the seat with their front legs over the coaming, and look out. When it wasn't actually raining Rommel stood longingly on one side or the other gazing at all that lovely land sliding past him at four knots.

Why, oh why didn't we stop and go ashore? A dog's proper place was on firm dry land. Couldn't I see that in persisting in travelling straight ahead, we stayed continuously on the water, when a tiny variation in course would land us? Until he got used to it, it was a source of great distress to him and on one or two occasions in Belgium, great frights – not to mention discomfort.

The second we touched shore his only thought was to get onto it immediately. He probably reasoned that if we had been so stupid as to ignore the land all day, then we were quite likely to be stupid enough to leave it again without giving him a chance for a moment on terra firma.

Boats come first. They have to be properly secured even on canals and rivers, there is always the danger that a passing barge will set you rocking and rolling in its wake, and if you're not securely tied up this can result in serious damage to the boat. Even dachsies have to take second place at these times, a lesson that Rommel had a hard time in learning.

Twice, early on in Belgium, Rommel tried to get himself ashore. He could just manage to climb out of the cockpit onto the narrow strip of deck outside it, but there wasn't much room there and whilst the rest of the boat had nylon netting along the sides there wasn't any at the stern because it would have interfered with various working ropes.

These attempts, made whilst our attention was otherwise occupied, resulted in a loud splash. A poor terrified head would appear between the boat and the shore, eyes rolling and he would try and climb vertically out of the water, up the side of the boat and back on board.

Needless to say the water in Belgium in April was near to freezing and the second time he fell in it gave him one of his favourite maladies – tonsillitis.

By the time we had diagnosed this we were on the outskirts of Nancy, home of the Dukes of Lorraine. Our French when we started had been limited to 'Bonjour' and 'Merci'. During the week or so we had transited Northern France I had added 'd'accord' to my vocabulary. This useful phrase could I found, be used in any circumstances at all – at least the French seem to.

Unfortunately none of these seemed likely to be of much help when trying to buy a course of antibiotics for a miniature dachshund with tonsillitis. I sent Jean to the chemist on the old principle of 'when in doubt delegate'.

I still consider that her success ranks second to mine in obtaining corn plasters for her and worm pills for the dogs in the same country. Corn plasters I have to confess were fairly simple and I managed the worms by wriggling my little finger. Jean of course, can draw – something I am quite incapable of. She is the sort of person who enjoys that revolting drawing game whose name I have no trouble in forgetting.

I presume she used the same methods, certainly later on she proved very successful with the Eastern European customs and immigration. She would go into the office, smile at everyone and shake all their hands, then spread out on the desk every official looking document which we possessed, finally she would produce a piece of paper and a pencil and very roughly draw Rainbow, the two dogs and a stick man and woman. Having done this she would sit down and beam at everyone with a satisfied smile. She claims that by the end of this performance everyone leapt to their feet, stamped everything in sight and ushered her nervously out of their offices lest this strange foreign madwoman should turn violent.

A couple of dips in water just off freezing taught Rommel his lesson, from then on he waited to be helped ashore, albeit a little impatiently.

In Europe we now encountered another problem. The dachsies are not urban dogs, their lives had been spent in places with large gardens with no-one else nearby, they had no idea of the pressures of urban living or the cultural adjustments necessary by the town dweller to oil their daily lives.

In Europe large dogs have become used to living cheek by jowl with other dogs, they have had to learn some tolerance. If they hadn't every street corner would be a gang warfare wasteland.

The dachsies had never had to learn this. If they were with us then it was obvious to them that we must be on our territory, it followed that any other dogs were intruders and should be attacked and with luck chased as far as possible. Offence was indicated especially as on a lead you could feel fairly sure that you would be restrained before you actually got within biting distance of anything very large.

The trouble with Rommel is that when he gets really excited he is liable to bite anything within range, including us. Bite is maybe a misnomer, Rommel works on the shark attack principle. That is he bares his teeth, opens his mouth and hurls himself at you, if you get in the way his teeth slice you open, he doesn't have to actually bite.

Jean is terrified of dog fights and of getting involved in one with Rommel. If she is walking him and sees another dog, she immediately reverses course, hides behind something, or failing other avenues of escape picks him up and covers his head so he can't see.

These methods are effective but there are lots of dogs in Europe, its hard to walk fifty yards without seeing one, nor is good cover always immediately available on city streets.

I would be chatting to Jean, vaguely notice another dog three hundred yards away, realise I was getting no reply and look round to find Jean with Rommel in her arms retreating at a run.

It was ridiculous.

I set out to teach both dogs and Rommel in particular, not to bark, snarl, growl and try and attack every passing dog. Teaching middle aged dachsies anything is not easy but at the end of nine months I had almost done it, he would actually walk past another dog with no more than a small token show of hackle.

In the process I got bitten on the chest and Jean got a tooth right through her thumb to the bone.

Jean's happened on the upper Danube in Austria.

We kept being told how beautiful the Wachau valley was in Austria, but in fact I far preferred the wilder upper Danube in Germany and the wide rolling, hazy, lazy river it became lower down in Eastern Europe.

In addition an Austrian in a power boat is a menace. Although the Austro-Hungarian Empire did have a small navy up to the First World War, as far as I know the last major naval engagement they were involved in was the battle of Lepanto, (the dogs have strolled on the same quays that the Turkish fleet was tied on the night before the battle). This was the last naval battle fought with galleys, where the object was to ram the opposition. This desire has apparently passéd into the Austrian psyche and remained unaltered for the last four hundred years or so.

Austria was also incidentally the only place in fifteen months that a private marina refused us permission to berth for the night. It was at the power boat club in Linz. We were told afterwards that it was a very snobbish club and presumably our appearance was not up to standard, but then we didn't want to go in, only to tie up to their jetty. As the club is sited up a dirty creek and surrounded by ship building yards it is not very salubrious either, but it rankled and even the kindness we met a short distance down stream at another club hasn't quite erased my ire.

None of which has anything to do with the evening when we tied up in an also rather unfriendly and very expensive marina in the Wachau. A man, not as far as I know even a boat owner, came down onto our jetty with a large Alsatian. He made not the slightest effort to control it and it came bounding along to where we were tied on alongside. Jean and I were walking back to the boat and Rommel was in the cockpit. It looked as if it was going to jump into Rainbow with him and Rommel in defence of his home can hardly be blamed for going berserk. He couldn't get out but he flung himself at the coaming in a wild fury whilst the Alsatian stood and barked at him from the jetty, about two feet away. Jean was in front of me and flung herself between the dogs and tried to push Rommel back, in the process he managed to bite her through her thumb.

The dogs were snarling and barking, there was blood everywhere and the Austrian owner some ten feet away ignored the whole thing from start to finish!

My bite occurred later in Istanbul.

I had him on a lead and was walking back along a jetty to Rainbow past a nine month old Labrador bitch. She was not only still young but a bitch and he had met her before so I didn't worry about her. It was a mistake. Rommel once again muddling his sexes went for her without any warning and she surprisingly retaliated. I picked him up to get him out of the way and promptly got bitten quite severely on my chest.

This inability of his to distinguish between sexes can be quite embarrassing. At the little city of Bamberg in Southern Germany on an early morning walk along the river he attempted to attack a very beautiful (and large) Alsatian bitch. When he got close the size difference rather overawed him and he stayed circling her at short range, growling fiercely. Fortunately she was nice natured and merely revolved slowly facing him and looking rather surprised.

Her owner, a very pretty girl was in hysterics.

"But he is a girl" she kept exclaiming "She is a dog, she must not bite girls!"

In Germany obviously dogs know who's what. I apologised and passed on, I felt my German was inadequate to deal with things like Rommel's poor sexual orientation.

Fenella never helped either. Whilst she has far too much sense to get involved with larger animals, she sees no reason why Rommel, being a male, shouldn't deal with them. Seeing another dog she will tear towards it barking madly, then stop ten yards away and maintain vocal encouragement for Rommel, whom she has started off, as of course she intended to.

I was glad to see later that Rommel was not alone in his attitude. The only other smooth haired dachsie we came across was, as I mentioned earlier, in the Greek islands, his owner being the wife of a local hotel owner and the waterman for the port.

"He is such a problem" she complained "when he was young he is no trouble, everybody know him and he walk around loose. Now he chase motorbikes and attack other dogs. We must tie him."

And so they did, later that day I was watching him sitting on the sun on the front step (tied) viewing the passing parade when an Alsatian walked past, he flung himself to the end of his tether in a futile and furious attempt to get at it and slaughter it.

At least it saved us a couple of pounds, which offset against the dogs food wasn't much. In Europe there was little choice except tinned dog's food. In Turkey, to the dogs' delight this was more expensive than fresh chicken – and chicken is what Fenella's like best!

The fairy tale German castles perched on crags along the Rhine, Main and Danube didn't (I don't think) impress the dachsies much, but there they met a new and satisfactory prey.

Not until May on the Main/Danube canal did the weather at last change for summer. Although we took the dogs walking regularly it was generally too damp and chilly for them to be very enthusiastic. Then finally it turned hot and sunny, and one day we locked up onto the European watershed, the High Jura, the continental divide, and found ourselves at the highest point of any waterway in Europe. From there on it was all downhill to the rolling swells of the Black Sea.

We breathed a sigh of relief and stopped the other side of the lock early in the afternoon for a deserved rest. There was a lock keeper's cottage and the lock keeper but not another soul or house in sight. On the far side of the canal the pine forest came down to the edge of the canal itself. On our side the land fell away in a smooth grass clad curve into a little valley. On the far side of this it rose gently to the edge of another evergreen forest. It was a beautiful clear sunny day, hot enough to be vaguely uncomfortable if you stayed out of the shade of our cockpit umbrella for too long.

I took the dogs ashore and set off for a proper walk. There was no one in sight, no road or other dangers so I didn't put them on their leads. We crossed the meadow and valley and followed a track into the pine woods. Fenella sniffling and smelling had lagged behind and Rommel was just in front of me when we came to a little clearing – and there sitting contentedly in a patch of sunlight in the centre was a RABBIT.

The rabbit and Rommel saw each other simultaneously; indecision seized them both, neither presumably ever having seen anything similar before. Both stood stock still about ten feet apart and considered each other nervously. I refrained from moving and watched.

Rommel made no move – what was it? Was it fierce? would it attack dachsies?

For its part the rabbit considered Rommel (it was a youngish rabbit) – what was this strange creature? It didn't look much like another rabbit although the size was about right and the colour not too far off, on the other hand it didn't look much like a dog or predator either. In short it was an animal new to a Bavarian rabbit – but was it anti-rabbit inclined?

For about five seconds the two contemplated each other.

Had the rabbit been the Wellington, Napoleon, Marlborough or Patton of its generation, who knows what rabbit lives it might have saved. It needed only to take a step out of character towards Rommel and he would probably have fled. Unfortunately it was only a run of the mill rabbit. Finally it followed rabbit law – when in doubt run.

The minute it did, Rommel established its place in the world – PREY. After it he went, albeit a little apprehensively at first. The rabbit being able to hop three feet to Rommel's one was soon lost in the woods. Rommel returned much interested, now the smell and sight of those things was known to him, he searched diligently for them thereafter, and rabbits paid the price. Whilst he never managed to catch an adult one, on a couple of occasions he discovered nests (burrows?) and slaughtered babies before he could be reached.

What lives that rabbit might have saved!

Fenella never had any doubts that they were dachsie prey from the first instant she saw one, and when she discovered that they lived in holes in the ground, she knew they were.

In Western Europe the canals and rivers tend to be heavily built up in most places and when we did stop all too often it was in places that required leads on the dogs. Also as I mentioned the weather was a little inclement, so the dogs didn't have much fun and being interested in neither history nor towns didn't have much compensation.

Once we started down the Danube, and the further down we got on our two and a half thousand kilometres to the Black Sea, things improved. Not only was it hot, in fact too hot a lot of the time, but lower down in Eastern Europe we usually anchored for the night by a deserted island or backwater. All too often every town you stopped at meant a two hour inspection by everyone ranging from the harbourmaster to the most secret police. Including on one occasion a gentleman who had obviously had a convivial lunch and, whilst extremely friendly, finally held me up for nearly an hour whilst he earnestly considered my passport upside down, and wondered what to do with it. To all intents and purposes every town was a border irrespective whether or not you had already cleared into that country.

Fortunately the lower Danube is a great beautiful hazy lazy river with islands and golden sandbanks, very few towns and only a few scattered villages. The odd fishermen in their flat bottomed square punt like boats, and barefoot shepherds herding cattle were the only people to be seen.

The dogs loved the sand spits and being able to take them ashore and let them run free gave them plenty of exercise. It was also warm enough so Fen could enjoy swimming. We were always very careful of her as she had never come across a current before and we had visions of her being swept down to the sea. Further down though, the river seldom flowed at more than two or three miles an hour and it was safe enough.

The first time she got caught in the current caused her great amazement. We were anchored in a little creek off the main stream behind an island with a long sand spit. Once we were firmly secured we took the dogs across to the island in the dinghy. On one side of the spit there was virtually no current, but on the other flowed the main stream. Jean and I were having a wash (Rainbow's facilities did not include running water much less showers) and Rommel was inland digging for animals when Fen swam out into the current. I saw her and called her back, she turned to swim to me, found she was going sideways, finally sorted it out and found that flat out she could just make headway. The expression of surprise on her face was comical – water had never behaved like this before!

Down in Eastern Europe, in Rumania and Bulgaria you don't find pets. The only dogs we saw, and not many of them, were working dogs. I have seen a lot of poverty in Africa but nothing to compare to up country Rumania at that time. When it is more than you can manage to feed yourself and keep yourself from freezing to death in winter, a pet would obviously be a mill stone around your neck. On one occasion I was in a post office on what was obviously welfare pay out day, it was filled with little old men and women, hunched, battered and toothless, dressed in rags and not one over four foot six inches tall. The shepherds we saw with the sheep wore no shoes and obviously had hardly ever done so.

We made a great friend down in Rumania later; he had played trombone in the Rumania State Orchestra for thirty years before he retired, but had never been able to own his own trombone. Yet Rumania, after Turkey, was the country we enjoyed the most. The people were friendly and hospitable and full of optimism for the future. We loved it, in Constanta on the Black Sea the streets are still named after Roman Emperors (in fact our friend's middle name was Octavian) and everyone had great pride in themselves and their history.

The poorer the country the more hospitable the people tend to be within their means – the rich are always too terrified that the stranger may be after a few of their shekels! Somewhere on the lower Danube there is a navigation launch with a little ebony head I gave them. They saw us arrive as strangers and insisted on our sharing their lunch.

Even here the dogs proved an excellent side show and caused much comment. One little barefoot boy of about ten was so taken with them that he insisted on walking round town with me for about two hours holding their leads.

We traversed the remains of war torn Yugoslavia where we had one of the most eerie experiences I can recall. On a hot sunny Sunday morning we came down the river to the city of Vukovar. From the distance there were the high rise buildings, cranes by the wharfs, streets. When we got close there were five Serb army men in a tent on the waterfront and high up in one block of flats some washing on a balcony. There was not another sign of life, no people, no cars, no buses or trucks just shell holes in every building and toppled cranes on the dockside. The scene could have come from a futuristic horror movie.

There was an inlet into a small inner harbour with a half sunken boat in it – the dogs needed a widdle and Jean pointed it out to me – we went on – no power on earth would have persuaded me to stop there.

This had unfortunate repercussions as further on there wasn't anywhere suitable to stop, finally I turned into the current and stemmed it, near a low island with sloping mud shores, Jean put the dogs into the Pot (our dinghy so named by a friend because it was always at the end of Rainbow) and paddled them ashore. They leapt out only to discover that the mud was more of a liquid consistency than solid. This might not have been so bad but then they saw that the low branches hanging over the river were alive with water rats. Even Rommel was prepared to swim in the interests of the hunt. Both of course were quiet deaf to Jean's yells to return to the dinghy. Finally she had to get out and try and catch them. The mud was about waste deep, by the time all were back in the dinghy everyone was black with mud from head to foot. Neither I nor the dogs were very popular for some days.

Serbia at the time was under United Nations sanctions with regard to fuel. At the border we were inspected by seven officials from seven different countries who carefully catalogued the seventy litres of diesel we carried in case we sold any in transit. For the next two hundred kilometres we watched the fishermen in their punts piled high with twenty litre cans ferrying fuel across the river from Rumania – on one occasion they even had fuel bowsers parked on both sides of the river opposite each other.

Naturally there were no patrols to stop it, but I think on occasion it might have been dangerous, once there was a massive explosion and cloud of smoke behind us and I am sure it was a careless fisherman with a cigarette.

At the other end of Serbia we were again inspected carefully by another multinational team to establish that we had used our diesel legitimately and not sold any!!

Finally we emerged on a blustery day into the great slow Black Sea rollers, put up our mast and made it through the Bosporus and Dardanelles down into the Aegean and Turkey where we spent that winter.

Our new mode of transport was not approved of by the dachsies. By now they definitely viewed Rainbow as home, but up to now it had been a stable one with the exception of one storm on the Danube. Home had now taken to performing in an unpleasant manner. One doesn't expect the floor of your home to tilt over twenty degrees and then go the other way, not to mention the front and back going up and down in the opposite directions.

Jean was in complete agreement with them but at least I didn't have her trying to climb on my lap all the time whilst I was steering. When we did meet bad weather all three tended to wedge themselves in a huddle on the cabin floor and remain there. When we both had to be outside we got vociferous complaints from the cabin. Naturally we couldn't risk letting them come up as if one had jumped or slipped overboard we would never have been able to find them even with their life jackets on.

Finally that winter we settled in a tiny fishing port, Kaynarpinar, in the Gulf of Izmir and life returned to more normal ways. We survived the winter, including a snow storm - a substance never before seen by either dog or indeed, Jean - but Fenella hardly emerged from the duvet for three months.

We loved Turkey and the Turks but the dogs had some unpleasant cultural shocks.

The first one was fish. The big twenty five metre Turkish trawlers and their ancillaries would pull into the nearest little fishing harbour at the end of each day to unload their catches. As the only little yacht around we stood out like a sore thumb and as they often came across us we soon knew nearly every crew. With the usual Turkish generosity whenever any were in port someone would bring us round a present of a small bag of the sardines which formed the bulk of their catch. Jean loathes all fish and won't eat it and I am not fond of it ad infinitum, but dog's food was expensive and I hate waste. It was impossible to refuse the gifts and anyway I felt it must be very good for the dogs' brainpower, so the dachsies got the bulk for supper. After a time even Rommel became disillusioned with it and Fenella viewed it with extreme disfavour.

I had to explain to them that we all had to make sacrifices on this trip and it was fish or nothing.

The major disillusionment, though, were the Turkish cats. There are a plethora of these in every harbour, living semi wild in the rocks of the breakwaters and surviving very adequately on fish and scraps. In Turkey the dogs are wimps and the cats the Kings of the Castles. I once saw a half grown kitten stroll up to and drive an adult Doberman off a piece of fish it fancied – it just walked up to it and gave it a left and a right to the nose. Turkish cats simply didn't behave in the way cats ought to when faced with dogs.

The first time the dachsies saw one sitting on a quay they were off in full flight towards it before we could stop them. Three foot away they slid to a stop, something was wrong.

Not only had the cat not run in the face of this noisy onslaught, but it hadn't even bothered to turn its head and look at them, much less stand up or make any movement. After a pause the dogs stopped barking at it and regarded it cautiously. It was certainly a cat, but attack it? It was in fact as big, if not bigger, than either of them.

There was a further brief hiatus then the cat condescended to turn it head over its shoulder and looked at them with an expression of mild surprise.

'What' it asked itself 'were these two peculiar looking animals? Not cats certainly and they made a noise like dogs, but if they were dogs what on earth did they think they were doing making that unseemly racket at a proper cat – and a Turkish one at that?'

The dachsies circled it giving the odd quavery and uncertain bark. Finally the cat stood up, stretched and strolled off in a leisurely manner on more important business.

'Ah' said the dachsies 'at last it's going to run away and we can give chase in the approved fashion'. Both made a dash at it in tongue. The cat neither speeded up nor bothered to look over its shoulder, the dachsies gave up and returned rather shamefaced.

After a few more of these encounters both adopted Rommel's approach to large dogs. They walked casually past watching them from the corners of their eyes. On the odd occasion when a cat ran they would be after it immediately. If it didn't they ignored it as if it didn't exist.

The cats could be really ferocious, later on separate occasions both dogs got attacked and Rommel badly cut up.

Each incident occurred when the dogs unwittingly stuck their noses into what I can only assume was a cathouse! In Rommel's case it was a large wooden box and the next thing I heard was howls of agony as he rolled on the ground with two cats on top of him with their claws latched into him. When I got there at a run they let go, but even then one stood its ground hissing and spitting at me.

Poor Rommel needed considerable first aid again and still has the battle scars.

Fenella got the same treatment later when she upset a nest in some rocks, she only got minor scars but the cats were coming out in relays, having a go at her, then dashing home again. Whether in both cases they had kittens or whether they merely objected violently to the invasion of their privacy I have no idea – I certainly wasn't going to stick my nose in to find out.

Chapter Eight

"Enter and look" said Peter then,
And send you well to speed.
But, for all that I know of women and men
Your riddle is hard to read.

Then flew Dinah from under the Chair
Into his arms she flew,
And licked his face from chin to hair
And Peter passed them through.'

R. Kipling

As I said we wintered that year in Kaynarpinar, I suppose it had a winter population of around sixty, one tiny shop and not much else.

We had also underestimated the Turkish winter, seeing snow for the first time might have been exciting, but huddled in Rainbow without electricity it was not always pleasant, and getting Fen out from the duvet required a lot of persuasion. This was especially true when the Northerly winds blew hard, the harbour, unlike many of the small fishing harbours, was safe and did not let in too heavy a swell, but the waves would break over the breakwater behind us throwing spray twenty feet into the air. This then blew across the quay onto us - getting off without getting soaked involved nimble footwork! but there were compensations.

Often there were sparkling sunny winter days and on these I would take the dogs walking in the hills. You could walk for miles along little footpaths and goat tracks without seeing a soul or hearing any sound except the whistle of the wind.

Grove after grove of olives with their silvery green leaves, little plantations of pine whose scent stung your nose and the endless six foot high Mediterranean scrub. Then the Turkish spring when every meadow blossomed into multicoloured sheets of wild flowers of every hue under the sun - and every size.

We would often walk up to eight or ten kilometres, at the same time climbing over a thousand feet and it would still take me half an hour to get warm, even wrapped in a sweater and anorak. Fen loved the walks and Rommel didn't mind too much but was always glad when we turned downhill again.

Most animals have an amazing ability to remember and find their way home, whether they are homing pigeons or mice in the Canadian Rockies, and neither is the ability bred out of dogs.

Years ago my parents had gone on long leave from Tanganyika and left our Alsatian Groucho with some missionaries they knew in our district. Colonial service leave in those days was for six months. He knew the people well and they were good with animals and anyway in those days there were no kennels he could have been left in.

When we came back and collected him they told us the story. He had stayed patiently waiting with them for about two weeks and then disappeared. At first hey thought that a wild animal had got him or he had strayed and got lost. Then reports started trickling in from around the district. Groucho appeared at every place he had been to with my father on safari, had a look, checked we were not there and gone on to the next. After two months he returned to the missionaries, battered, half starved but alive and settled down with them to wait until we returned.

How he found his way to places he had only visited in a car, how he survived (he had a habit of chewing stones and had practically no teeth left) we will never know. My father calculated that he must have covered in the region of six hundred miles through unpopulated bush, somehow keeping himself alive and avoiding larger predators.

Fenella amazed me in Kaynarpinar, we only had to go on a walk once and she would remember it. Running ahead if she came to a junction she would pause looking down the track which led to the shortest way home, then look back at me.

I only had to say "That's right, we'll take that one" and off she would go down it, or "No we're going the other way" and off she would go down that one.

It was wild hilly country and the paths zigzagged up the hillsides at a gradient suitable for the mules and donkeys which provided much of the internal transport there. She would disappear from behind me then re-appear on the track ahead having taken a direct route between zigzags. How she knew, especially if it was the first time we had walked that way, was a mystery as the scrub was nearly impenetrable and when she left me I was often walking in the opposite direction.

I can only think that dachsies use stones and tree roots in the same way we might take bearings from mountain peaks. I could have put her down anywhere in those hills and I am certain she would have come home unerringly to Rainbow.

We tended to think that Africa was bad for burrs, prickles and spiky plants but the Mediterranean shores can be far worse. Fen used to pick up a few scratches on her tummy occasionally but it never worried or stopped her. Poor Rommel was another matter.

After he had scratched himself a few times he approached any low growth at the pace of an aged and crippled tortoise. Closing his eyes in anticipation of the agony to come, he would push his head slowly through the obstruction, followed by one leg at a time and his body. His whole attitude resembled a nervous apprentice fire walker on his first outing. Once on the other side he would pause a second open his eyes and ask himself "Have I received any serious injury, cuts, abrasions or damage?"

Only when satisfied that he was still in one piece would he continue. Not infrequently he would consider himself stuck and I would have to come and rescue him. Rommel is not made of the material of great explorers.

Since we left the Danube either conditions had been unsuitable or the weather had been too cold for the dogs to be interested in water. Although Rommel won't swim unless pressed he does like to stand up to his tummy in water to cool off when he's hot. At last spring and summer returned and one day coming back from our walk it was actually hot, and so were the dogs.

They made a beeline for the beach, plunged in and took a refreshing drink.

Ugh" they both said "there's something seriously wrong with this water".

Rommel had another look. Water wasn't nice but at least in his experience it had always been drinkable, he had another taste, it still tasted the same. Fenella seldom drinks much but Rommel does. When we finally left and returned to Zimbabwe, he was still trying to drink seawater.

I suppose it was logical. He knows water is drinkable and probably assumes that this is simply a place with bad water. On the other hand as we were continually moving day after day to different places, surely it couldn't be salty and undrinkable everywhere? You have never seen a dog wear an expression of such disgust each time to he sampled it.

We spent an idyllic spring and early summer passing down the Turkish coast, across to Greece through the Corinth canal from the deep purple Aegean to the pale blue Ionian seas and round the coasts of both countries. New places to explore, new smells every day, they were halcyon days.

Only three incidents remain with me, one funny, one alarming and one which demonstrates that aliens from other worlds smell the same to dogs as do ordinary people.

The meeting with an alien took place on a particularly wild stretch of Turkish coast. We had found an inlet, shallow enough to anchor, completely deserted, no buildings and safely weather protected. It was heavenly, so much so that we stayed there about three days.

The first day we arrived just before lunchtime. Jean was listening at that time to a BBC programme in which some man said that aliens were among us but would be leaving shortly. If you wished to contact one, he said, it was only necessary to write or beam a message giving a rendezvous and time and usually if you went there one would turn up.

About 4pm. I was down in the cabin doing some typing when to my amazement I heard Jean having a conversation with someone in English. First of all there was no-one else there and secondly this was far off any beaten track, tourist or otherwise, and you did not often find anyone speaking anything but Turkish.

I stuck my head up and found she was talking to one of the itinerant goat herds. These are employed to look after perhaps two or three hundred goats; they move them almost daily up and down the coast living in small temporary shacks of poles and tarpaulins. This one, a middle aged man spoke faultless accent-less English, although his vocabulary was not enormously wide

He moved on with his goats and I went back down below. Jean looked down into the cabin and said "Just look under the typewriter. I looked and found a folded piece of paper, on it she had written 'If there are any aliens around please will one come and speak English to me by four o'clock."

Of course it was all nonsense! In the next few days I came across him a few times when I was walking the dogs and chatted to him. Every time I returned Jean would ask "Did you ask him what world he came from."

Of course I didn't, he might have changed shape, grown antenna and turned green in front of my eyes! I didn't feel that the fact the dogs didn't seem to think there was anything strange about him was any guarantee, after all aliens presumably could deceive dogs as well as people!

Two other men used to come down on an aged tractor and trailer in the evenings to help him milk the herd and to take the milk away. One day he asked me to come along and said he would give me some of the milk. At that time of the year, he said, the goats were eating the buds on shrubs and the milk was superb.

I paddled over in the dinghy one dusk.

The goats were corralled on a steep hillside. In a narrow gap in the stone wall the three men sat shoulder to shoulder, milked a goat, shoved it up above them and let another one in. Cigarettes trailed from the corners of their mouths. It was a scene almost biblical. Then I looked up and found a goat which had been milked standing on a rock just above me, it was leaning forward and sucking air in through widened nostrils. They laughed - it was addicted to tobacco smoke and I was smoking my pipe! The milk poured into blackened containers through dubious looking muslin made me a little nervous, but he was right it was nectar, almost as if honey had been added but without the sweetness.

The funny one took place on the boat.

I was standing in the galley cooking one day when I heard a thump behind me, looking round I saw my anorak walking across the floor towards me, one arm and pointing inexorably at me. For a second I was frozen with horror and wondered whether we had acquired some type of poltergeist or if I was being subjected to some inexplicable occurrence originating from another dimension.

Then I bent down and peeled back that pointing cuff and revealed the end of a small black nose. Fen had been curled up on it, and when she got down had somehow gone up (down?) one sleeve. She fitted it almost perfectly but unfortunately the cuff was too small to allow her to emerge – hence the walking jacket!

The third happened on Jean's birthday anchored in a quiet bay on the West coast of Greece, Fenella swallowed a fishhook complete with line. We could never afford steak, but had bought some for this occasion and Jean had used a tiny bit of gristle to put on a fish hook.

I cut the line leaving about eighteen inches hanging out of her mouth. The hook was firmly embedded and I couldn't reach it or the lead sinker. Then she swallowed the rest of the line! There was no vet there so at three in the morning we headed or Corfu thirty miles away.

There we found a vet, had her X-rayed and there was the hook clearly showing halfway down her throat.

Later I discovered that fish hooks are made of very poor quality metal and left alone the digestive juices will probably dissolve them in a matter of days. I didn't know it then so I let them operate. It seemed simple, but it wasn't, after and hour they couldn't find it and gave up. They said it must have moved. Jean and I were in despair, the operation had been a major one and there was no way she could face another - as it was it took her some time to recover. Wherever it was, there was nothing further we could do about it.

Three weeks later she coughed up the fishing line and I cut it off as short as I could. The line had worried me a much as the hook, as being nylon it wouldn't have dissolved. For some time she had an occasional cough, then that passed and since then she has never shown any sign of a problem. I can only assume that the hook rotted and the remainder of the line passed through. I only wish that I hadn't let them operate in the first place. She had an awful time as they had kept her on a very light anaesthetic and from then on if she saw a man in a white coat she fled in terror.

Before we left Africa the dogs had always been fed on fresh meat, in Europe this was often impossible or else simply too expensive and they got tinned (except for the fish), but we also bought them dog biscuits which they hadn't had before. Fenella developed a passion for these. We gave them to her after supper and soon she would demand them as soon as she had finished.

For some reason she appeared to believe that you only got a biscuit if you had earned it or something unusual had happened. She began searching for excuses, first she decided that a long walk warranted some and would demand them on her return. Finally anything unusual would be considered an excuse. She would stand on the seat with her nose pointed at the compartment in which they were kept, give a yelp, look at Jean and then turn her nose pointedly in the direction of the biscuits.

Occasionally for one reason or another we would move them to a different compartment and it would take a few days for her to catch on and go to the right place.

What with Fenella's operation and dog biscuits money seemed to be sliding through our fingers and at last the day came when Jean and I looked at each other and agreed we had to stop before we ran out completely.

Jean and the dachsies flew back to Zimbabwe from Athens and I followed via England so I could see my parents. At least this time the dogs were on the same plane as Jean, they also had their uses.

Jean collected them straight off the plane in Harare, they were both in their kennels on a trolley with all her luggage. By this time naturally she was at the end of the queue. Zimbabwe Customs and Immigration officials are not generally known either for their pleasant attitude, courtesy or efficiency and getting through can be a long slow process.

Not for Jean though - the dogs had had enough of kennels, planes and being cooped up. Jean says the noise was indescribable. Within minutes an official had whisked her out of the queue, through the formalities at a run, out of the airport and into the car park.

"Don't bring them back in" he said firmly and left her there.

EPILOGUE

'Come let us draw the curtains,
And talk of other things,
And presently all will be quiet,
Love, youth and the sound of wings.'

Anon

What on earth did the dachsies make of it all? We will never know but they are remarkably resilient even though Fenella is twelve now and Rommel only a year younger but going grey.

Some things were confusing. Sometimes Rainbow would be moored stern on to the quay and you went to the back to get off, then she would be alongside or bows on. Fenella would jump on the stern only to find nothing but water there. All these changes were hard to keep up with!

Then there was the current in the Danube, and later that peculiar tasting salty water, not to mention unaccustomed cold and wet.

The only lasting behaviour pattern caused by it all is Fenella's and has nothing to do with the trip. It arose from the two months she spent in kennels before we could get them to Europe.

Year by year now every new animal study debunks that old belief that animals are dumb, unthinking, unreasoning things and could be treated as inanimate objects. Not that I suppose knowing this will change many attitudes in view of the way humans treat other humans. We will probably never know to what extent they can measure time, but certainly they can tell meal times and the difference between, short, medium and long periods, and two months locked in a kennel is a *long period*.

No doubt totally erroneously, I believe she reasoned along these lines.

'I know he loves me and I love him so he would never willingly abandon me in that place. The only explanation is that something else caught him and locked him up so that he couldn't get back to release me. Therefore I mustn't let him out of my sight in case it catches him again when I'm not there to protect him.'

The result is that she won't leave me. If Jean tried to take her for a walk and I was on the boat, about fifty yards was the furthest she would go before digging her heels in and refusing to budge an inch. Even now two years later she is the same. If I'm not at home she will go with Jean, but if I'm there she won't even leave the room.

Rommel, of course remains unperturbed by it all – visibly that is.

Only the very famous or infamous have their biographies written in their lifetime, and I, despite prejudice, cannot claim that either Rommel or Fenella fall into these categories. It was simply that I woke up one night with Fen snuffling sleepily on my shoulder and thought how much pleasure and joy (not to mention high blood pressure) they have given us and how much we love them. I wanted to record it now for our own memories later, assuming of course that they predecease us which is by no means certain.

An American woman writer about dogs was once asked if she believed that dogs went to Heaven, "Of course" she replied unhesitatingly "Otherwise there wouldn't be a heaven."

Its how I feel – only our daughters will never forgive me. For years they have said "You love Fenella more than us!", now they will add "I bet you couldn't write a book about us when we were young, you'd never remember all those little things."

In mitigation I can only beg their pardon and say in my defence that neither of them have such fine silky, shiny black fur or such a long elegant Roman nose.

Maybe there are better trained dogs, more famous dogs, more adventurous dogs, more intelligent dogs but there can't be many better travelled dogs.

Zimbabwe, Zambia, Malawi, Egypt, Holland, Belgium, France, Germany, Austria, Slovakia, Hungary, Serbia, Romania, Bulgaria, Turkey and Greece. Thousands of miles by road in Africa and by river, canal and sea in Europe.

The rivers – Aisne, Somme, Meuse, Rhine, Main and two and half thousand kilometres of the great blue Danube. The seas – British Channel, North Sea, Black Sea, Sea of Marmara, Aegean Sea, Ionian Sea and the Adriatic.

The Bosporus, Golden Horn and Dardanelles.

In a town called Cannakale in the latter we hired a car and took the dogs to visit the ruins of Troy, a city so mythical that its very existence was doubted, and so real that it existed eight thousand years ago.

I don't think the dachsies were too impressed. Three bus loads of large German tourists arrived simultaneously and most of the tour was taken up in an effort to avoid being trampled to death. It was a pity because had it been empty they would have loved it. Jumbles and piles of old rocks and old stones everywhere – it looks like Fenella's idea of ideal lizard hunting country.

Still like Ulysses, Agamemnon, Achilles, Paris, Helen, Xerxes of Persia, Alexander the Great and three million German tourists, Rommel Lousada and Fenella Lousada can boast that they have been to Troy.

POSTSCRIPT

'Under the wide and starry sky
Dig the grave and let me lie:
Glad did I live and gladly die
And I laid me down with a will.

This be the verse that you grave for me:
Here he lies where he long'd to be:
Home is the sailor, home from the sea,
And the hunter home from the hill.'

R. L. Stevenson

Fenella died in Harare in the RSPCA kennels in the early hours of the morning of Thursday 21st August 1997. She was not with me and I still blame myself bitterly, although, there was nothing I could have done about her death anyway.

Rommel died at a town called Chinhoyi at 11am on the morning of 6th August 1998.

I have never quite forgiven myself about Fenella.

What happened was this. We had kept Rainbow in Greece – she was in fact the only thing we possessed, also things were slowly going from bad to worse in Zimbabwe and I had a feeling that we might one day need her for a roof over our heads. Which in fact we did in 2003.

Boats like houses need looking after, airing and checking out. Also we loved the Ionian and the Greek islands. Every year after we left, we managed to save just enough money to fly over to Greece and spend about four weeks on Rainbow, once there of course our costs were minimal.

That year, 1997, we had booked and paid for cheap flights to Athens in August, then about five days before we left we noticed that Fen was listless and unwell although not apparently in any discomfort. We took her to our local vet who diagnosed a form of tick bite fever, gave her an injection and assured us that she would be fine in a few days.

We were living in a town on the Eastern border called Mutare and had to drive some three hundred miles to Harare to catch our flight. We had arranged to leave the dogs in the RSPCA kennels in Harare. They had stayed there before and we knew the woman managing it and she was excellent.

We drove through a day before the evening of our flight, and it was apparent that Fen was not only not better but much worse, and the car journey made her sick, something that had never happened before.

We took them into the kennels and consulted our friend who immediately booked us an appointment with a firm of vets which she said were the best in town. We took her there, they examined her very thoroughly, took numerous blood samples and rushed them to laboratories.

The next morning we went back, they had found not a trace of any disease or anything wrong. The vet assured us that it was simply a very bad stomach upset, gave her an injection and a course of pills and assured us with complete confidence that in twenty-four hours she would be fine. Fen herself didn't seem to be in any pain or discomfort just very tired and listless.

We didn't know what to do. The tickets we had could neither be changed or refunded, if anyone stayed it would have been me and Jean wouldn't go on her own. The vet had been so thorough and so confident that nothing serious was wrong that we discussed it with he kennel lady, who we knew could be trusted to keep a close eye on her, and to my shame we went.

For some reason that I cannot recall we had to go via England and we spent a night in Cairo en route. The next evening when we were in Heathrow we phoned Harare, expecting to hear she was fine only to be told that she had died during the previous night.

The woman said she was so sorry, she had really seemed better in the evening and had eaten well and she hadn't been worried at all and simply checked on her the first thing the next morning only to find her dead.

For many years I have not even been able to think about it, now, although I find it of little comfort, I can at least recognise that there were some factors that mitigated my absence.

She died with Rommel whom she loved and who had been with her all her life, and I don't think she suffered. She died from internal bleeding but no-one ever managed to tell us what caused it.

The third one is so fanciful, and for that matter so easily explained, that I am not quite sure I believe it. In Egypt that night we had twin beds. Some time in the early hours of the morning I woke believing that Fenella was sleeping by my side. I didn't move so as not to disturb her and went back to sleep. It is easy to imagine that I was so used to her there that my mind, half asleep, played a trick on me – but – I don't know, I can still recall how physical the sensation was. Anyway sometimes I like to think that her love transcended distance and that when she was dieing she also thought herself with me.

Poor Rommel at least died in my arms.

We were managing a motel at the time and that morning Jean and I were standing outside chatting to a guest and Rommel was wandering round as usual poking his nose into things when he suddenly started banging his head on the ground. Within seconds his tongue had swollen to twice its size.

We rushed him down to the local vet who was unfortunately away, however his assistant did her best, but within about fifteen minutes he had lapsed into unconsciousness and died shortly after.

Whatever it was had obviously bitten him on the tongue, whether it was simply a bee or wasp I don't know, but the effects were so violent that I think he probably disturbed a small snake.

He is buried beside Fenella in a quiet grave under trees in a corner of the RSPCA complex in Harare.

If they have not been stolen, each has a small plaque with their names and dates of birth and death on it. One of the last things we did before we let Zimbabwe for good in 2003 was to visit them.

Also on the plaque are two lines borrowed from Stevenson, so apt that I am sure he would not have grudged us their use:-

"Home is the sailor, home from the sea,
And the hunter home from the hill."

THE END